Joyful, Anyway

ALSO BY KATE BOWLER

*Blessed: A History of the
American Prosperity Gospel*

*Everything Happens for A Reason
(And Other Lies I've Loved)*

*The Preacher's Wife: The Precarious
Power of Evangelical Women Celebrities*

*No Cure for Being Human
(And Other Truths I Need to Hear)*

*Good Enough: 40ish Devotionals
for a Life of Imperfection
(with Jessica Richie)*

*The Lives We Actually Have:
100 Blessings for Imperfect Days
(with Jessica Richie)*

*Have a Beautiful, Terrible Day!:
Daily Meditations for the Ups,
Downs & In-Betweens*

Joyful, Anyway

Kate Bowler

BLOOMSBURY TONIC
LONDON · OXFORD · NEW YORK · NEW DELHI · SYDNEY

BLOOMSBURY TONIC
Bloomsbury Publishing Plc
50 Bedford Square, London, WC1B 3DP, UK
Bloomsbury Publishing Ireland Limited,
29 Earlsfort Terrace, Dublin 2, D02 AY28, Ireland

BLOOMSBURY, BLOOMSBURY TONIC and the Tonic logo are
trademarks of Bloomsbury Publishing Plc

First published in 2026 in the United States by The Dial Press,
an imprint of Penguin Random House LLC
First published in Great Britain in 2026

Copyright © Kate Bowler, 2026

Kate Bowler is identified as the author of this work in accordance with the
Copyright, Designs and Patents Act 1988

Interior art: pages 11, 110, 222, and 250 (handwriting) and pages 62 and 153
(Venn diagrams) by Kateri Kramer

All rights reserved. No part of this publication may be: i) reproduced or
transmitted in any form, electronic or mechanical, including photocopying,
recording or by means of any information storage or retrieval system without prior
permission in writing from the publishers; or ii) used or reproduced in any way for
the training, development or operation of artificial intelligence (AI) technologies,
including generative AI technologies. The rights holders expressly reserve this
publication from the text and data mining exception as per Article 4(3) of the
Digital Single Market Directive (EU) 2019/790

Bloomsbury Publishing Plc does not have any control over, or responsibility for,
any third-party websites referred to in this book. All internet addresses given in
this book were correct at the time of going to press. The author and publisher
regret any inconvenience caused if addresses have changed or sites have ceased to
exist, but can accept no responsibility for any such changes

A catalogue record for this book is available from the British Library

ISBN: HB: 978-1-0372-0256-8; TPB: 978-1-0372-0257-5; eBook: 978-1-0372-0258-2

2 4 6 8 10 9 7 5 3 1

Book design by Jo Anne Metsch
Printed and bound in Great Britain by Clays Ltd, Elcograf S.p.A

To find out more about our authors and books visit www.bloomsbury.com and
sign up for our newsletters
For product-safety-related questions contact productsafety@bloomsbury.com

This book is dedicated to all the swifties.
May we be glued together by more than saliva.

Q. What is joy?

Circle the following correct answer:

a. fireworks that light us up from within

b. a relief from "the ache"

c. a gift our hearts are made for

d. a moment in the midst of nothing terribly special

e. an interruption to our usual lives

f. an emotional version of spontaneous combustion

g. a stranger that needs to be invited in

h. the only way to feel truly alive

i. deepest hope and delight and gratitude

j. all of the above

AUTHOR'S NOTE

IN SHARING THESE memories, I have sometimes blended characters or changed names and details to protect the privacy of those involved. My intention is to honor their stories as well as their confidentiality. Because, in the end, a big part of joy is keeping your friendships intact.

CONTENTS

Prologue: The Music   1

PART I: THE ACHE

1. Joyful, Except on Tuesdays   9
2. The Ache   17
3. Things I Worry I Will Not Survive: An Incomplete List   24
4. Hungry, Hungry Hippos   26
5. The Basement   29
6. I Asked Strangers on the Internet What They Ache For: A List   33
7. Ashes Than Dust   35
8. The House   43
9. What Causes the Ache: An Incomplete List   48
10. Toxic Positivity   50

CONTENTS

11	The Formula That Solves Everything	56
12	Fantastic Ideas I've Already Tried to Solve the Ache	63
13	The Algorithm	65
14	Is This It?	68

PART II: MOURNING

15	Swifties	77
16	The List: Recent Filings to the Complaints Department	88
17	Anybody?	90
18	This Is Not Codependency	94
19	Highly Sensitive People	99
20	Poisonous Pedagogy	108
21	The Leaky Heart	113
22	Below Sea Level	116
23	Pruning Shears	119
24	Friend-Tested Rituals for Processing the Everythingness of Life: A List	131
25	Prescription from Henry	136

PART III: JOY

26	A Few Quick Questions Before I Fill a Prescription for Joy	143
27	Ta-da!	145
28	Joy (According to Researchers)	154

CONTENTS

29	Puzzle Corners	156
30	Joy (According to the Grief-Stricken)	159
31	Trash Walks	161
32	Joy (According to Kids I Know)	168
33	Hallelujah	169
34	Sideburns	174
35	Microjoys: Tiny Delights People Reported to Me This Week	177
36	Made for You	179
37	Among the Trees	186
38	The Nurse	194
39	Off the Edge	204
40	Ways to (Almost) Guarantee Joy for No Reason	213

PART IV: LIVING

41	The Biggest Tiny Thing You Can Do	219
42	Expect a Miracle	224
43	God Bless Us Everyone	229
44	Surprising Moments Other People Have Found Joy: A List	235
45	The Task	238
46	Ways I Have Been Tasked with Love Lately: An Incomplete List	251
47	Ka-boom	253
48	The Song	262

THE MUSIC

IT SHOULD NEVER have happened. Who gets married *outside* in Minnesota in late October? The wedding was a blur of high heels and tailored suits and guests shivering under enormous coats while my college roommate, the bride, wore an insane sleeveless dress she had picked out with her mom. I was a bridesmaid in a thin turquoise sateen without a shawl so I insisted that I suffered the most for having to face the crowd with a smile plastered on my face, but, in truth, the view was spectacular. The bride's mother sat in the front row with tears streaming down her cheeks, her husband resting his arm around her shoulder as if tethering her to him. She looked like a woman genuinely awed by seeing so much returned to her, as if there had been some miracle confirmed in watching her daughter confidently saying her vows, radiant with joy.

And it should never have happened—the funeral that soon followed, the way death showed his face on some insignificant afternoon and took the mother of the bride with him. A car accident. She was there and then she was gone, leaving her family with the paperwork and the robocalls and the Facebook account that could not be taken down. A modern death is a digital haunting, a never-finished flurry of notifications. I do not pretend to know where to find the key that unlocks the mystery between mothers and daughters, but I know that sometimes two people stare at each other and see only their reflection. They can talk and fight and scream and say things like "You always..." and "You never..." but they never quite break the glass between them. Now my friend's mother was dead and what went unspoken between them could drown the ocean.

I have known days like these, days full of dragging sadness. I was thirty-five years old when I was diagnosed with incurable Stage IV cancer. I had married my high school sweetheart, finally had a son after years of infertility, and secured my dream job as a university professor—then, suddenly, every hope had to be placed back on the shelf. I lived for years assuming that each season would be my last. It's hard for those who haven't lived with it to understand the feelings that coexist with existential terror. From one moment to the next, I could only expect that *anything* might happen. I might feel genuinely terrified about my life, which was unraveling. Or lulled into boredom in every waiting room. Or I might think I was going to finally get back to work, only to use up all my energy trying to get my hair into a decent ponytail without pressing down on the wretched IV on the back of my hand.

Years later, I had mostly made it through the fog and I was watching my friend, that grieving bride, make her own perilous way forward, able to see only a couple of feet in front of her. I wanted to tell her what I had learned from that time of my life that had been marked by grief—the unforgettable period sticky with Jell-O and the specter of death. I wanted to give her a promise that reasonable people would be too reluctant to guarantee, but it is one I would hang my life on: *You will never be cured of this grief, it's true. But you will be joyful, anyway. I swear.*

When a loss of any kind—breakup, breakdown, or any terrible undoing—descends upon your life, joy seems to vanish. The vibrancy that once filled your days fades, leaving the world colorless and cold. This sudden shift doesn't simply numb; it transforms everything around you. Laughter feels strange and a sense of ease is a distant memory. In this new reality, even the smallest spark of joy seems impossible to ignite. And even worse, suggested the nineteenth-century philosopher Søren Kierkegaard, joy becomes the source of suffering. Its memory stokes the fires of hurt. The joy we once had, the joy we remember, becomes our ruin. It is not so much lost as missed, he wrote. When you are in the deep abyss of grief, sadness, or, worst of all, despair, joy feels like an insult.

"I am barely okay," my friend said tearfully, "and now you're trying to convince me that I could feel euphoric. Are you insane?!"

At that we both cracked a smile, which turned into a long stretch of making jokes about me. Wasn't I the person who recently insisted that we take a three-hour detour to visit the world's largest turtle made of spare tires? Hadn't I organized a walking contest that dislocated a friend's hip while everyone was forced to dress like Dolly Parton? Was I really to be trusted?

But I know about the joy that persists, even though it might seem like temporary insanity.

I looked at my friend, red eyes and water-stained shirt, and I could see how impossible joy felt to her. In fact, not long ago, I would not have believed in joy either. It's strange to say it like that—but I *believe in joy*. We can't mistake it for anything less than what it is: one of the most powerful ways we experience the deepest and most healing forms of gratitude, delight, and hope. It is a kind of transcendence; joy is a glimmer of love and forgiveness and wholeness that lifts us out of reality for a moment and gives us back to ourselves, anew.

At first, in my own life, joy appeared as an incredible reversal—I should have been devastated, but then its bright light appeared. Joy came to me like a rush of love that bubble-wrapped me for weeks at a time. It came to me a moment before surgery and every time I threw a taste-test party. Joy felt like a miracle.

But then I survived cancer and life was just life again: meetings and to-do lists and errands and follow-up appointments, wrestling an iPad away from my son and arguing with my husband about who is actually reading the endless school emails with a hidden code to log in to a magical portal that forces me to continue the educational journey until bedtime. I was languishing. I kept thinking that I should feel grateful for all of it, but mostly I felt bored, sometimes annoyed, and then, inevitably, guilty. But soon I discovered that joy is there, too—in the ordinary—if you are willing to take the chance.

If you ask people who have really gone through something—the people who have been wrung out from their insides and forced to act the part of normal human beings on the outside—

they might tell you about joy and how there is nothing predictable about it. Sometimes, often, they were devastated, but then, curiously, there were moments that went beyond okayness. They worried that they could never be happy again but—what's that?—there it was: joy.

"There are always two preachers at a funeral." Death and Hope. That's what my friend Tom Long likes to say. There will be a body, and then there needs to be a person who stands up to tell the story about the love that goes on and on.

There will always be a body. There will always be a world on fire. Despair is a powerful preacher. But then, wait a minute, I think I hear a song.

Like birds singing.

It does not cry: *Is this it?*

It insists: *There is more.*

The newspaper headlines will agree that there is nothing worth being joyful about. Everywhere is cancer, hurricanes, stock market disasters, and teenage anxiety disorders. Let's not forget troll farms, conspiracy theories, and drone strikes. We hear the steady drumbeat of the looming apocalypse but there is so much important shrugging to be done in the meantime. A new study emerges every year documenting the sinkhole of mistrust underneath most public institutions but, fingers crossed, someone official is still testing the strength of highway bridges. Who can save us anyway when we are swimming in microplastics and forever chemicals?

It feels, argues the theologian Charles Mathewes, like we're experiencing a global withering of our capacity for joy.

But then again . . .

Has anyone looked closely at the eyelashes on babies? Ridiculous. I mean, useless. But delightful. Every weekend some Good Samaritans I know have been rehabbing church basements to house families who have no other place to stay. Before I fall asleep I like to replay the scene where a friend of mine competed in a well-attended dog show as a human contestant. She hit all her marks and jumped through a hoop two feet off the ground.

I have been reading Jack Gilbert poems lately and I keep returning to his classic "A Brief for the Defense," which catalogs the atrocities of the world. He lands on this stunning admission: "We must admit there will be music despite everything."

It's true. We can hear the music despite everything. And we have to sing it over and over and over again.

In the many chambers of our beating hearts are reservoirs for joy.

"You will hear the music," I said to my friend. "I swear you will hear the music."

PART
I

The Ache

I

Joyful, Except on Tuesdays

THE ALARM STARTS blaring and I'm up. I'm up now.

Through the grainy dark, across the bedroom, I see the door crack open and stop abruptly. Then a figure turns sideways and slips through. For months I have been trying to give away a blanket that looks like a lightly toasted burrito, which undermines my living room's attempts to be sufficiently midcentury modern. But, rather mysteriously, the blanket continues to disappear from the Give-Away Box and here it is, floating like a phantom through the dark until it pauses by my bed.

The burrito wedges himself under the duvet and sighs.

"What did you dream about, Mom?" hisses my son, Zach, because he can't possibly whisper.

"I dreamed I was being pulled behind an enormous boat and I couldn't let go," I tell him, and glance toward the bedside table. My phone is blinking with a reminder about the "no lateness" policy at my Pilates class as tardiness disturbs the vibrational atmosphere. And below that is a WhatsApp message letting me know that while I was sleeping there was a flurry of classroom moms who needed someone—but who?—to bring gluten-free cookies for the fundraiser. I read both a few times over to make sure I am not still in the fugue state of sleep medication. Ever since chronic pain and cancer made their sudden appearance way back when, I don't so much fall asleep as need to be *put to sleep* like a tranqued bear. I put my head back under the sheets.

Lately the number of small obligations and small heartaches—the sheer volume of them—makes me feel like I can't breathe. Like every thought about what I *should do* races from my head to my heart to my lungs. Then every thought about what I *can't do* constricts my chest for a moment. Every time I allow myself to fully consider the direction my life is taking, I feel a little shock wave running through me. But soon I'll get up, make breakfast, and take a lot of fish-oil vitamins with the chilling guarantee of "minimal burp-backs" and that will allow me to limit a normal intake of self-esteem for the day.

"Don't worry about the dream," says the boy, burrowing deeper into his tortilla wrapping. "It's like cupping water in my hands in the bath. It slips away." He says it exactly like that, those precise words, like a seasoned meditation instructor. Then he adds: "Also I have learned that grenades are very simple devices. Is there a place where children can practice using grenades?"

He has been enthusiastically ignoring our family's commitment to pacifism for some time now.

I hear the sound of the coffee grinder downstairs and feel a wave of gratitude for this off-ramp. My son feels my attention shifting and wraps his arms tighter around me.

"Please consider today if we can buy a zeppelin," he says, and I resolve to have another word with my father about whether he can lay off military history in his nightly Zoom chats with his grandson. *How about cultivating an appreciation for nature?* I will say, and my dad will invariably reply that air-conditioning is God's promise that we never need to go outside again.

By the time I have put on my jeans and a blazer, waterproof mascara, grabbed my gym bag, and made some hurried but uninterpretable sounds of thanks to my husband for the coffee, I'm out the door.

Good habits are the foundation of everything, so I start the weekday morning like every other. I sit down at my desk with a hot cup of hazelnut creamer and a splash of coffee, a heating pad for my old-man back, and a feverish delusion that I will claw my way out of the overflowing garbage heap that is my inbox and list of tasks.

- Call the pharmacy again about the prescription.

- Scratch that. First message the Doctor about the Refill for that Prescription

- You'll need the password for the hospital Messaging system to contact that doctor. Start the password recovery process

- Give a mouse a cookie

Never mind. I'll do it later. Errands are never errands. Errands are the referendum on whether I have enough of my nervous system left over to restart a fight with Linda from HR about a billing error. Sometimes I get the distinct impression that my feelings are not actually my own. I have been plugged—*Matrix*-style—into the parasympathetic circuitry of the universe.

I run through today's litany of activities: praying for the Best Friend's dumb relationship, waiting on my mammogram result for a suspicious lump, worrying about someone who is irritated with me (I think, not sure), and calling my mom to ask about her gum graft surgery while pretending that I am also recovering from my own gum graft surgery to see if I can make her feel sorry for *me*. But that's just for fun. And of course there's my actual job: grading, research, faculty meetings, interviewing for my podcast, and writing, writing, writing.

After an hour or so, the mania has subsided. Digging into some historical research gives me the strange synchronized calm of a woman in motion. I have always been quieted by work, squeezed into the wonderful necessity of what is in front of me. At the very least, it *feels* necessary, and that feeling turns down the volume on the deafening needs of everyone around me. Marriage made me a wife, my son made me a mother, and cancer made me a feminist. Had I not been diagnosed, I never would have turned up the sound of my own screaming desires. Not that anyone else heard them scream. I think, in the end, I mostly sounded like I was politely clearing my throat.

It has been ten years since that diagnosis, which is a shocking gift. And now that I am technically cancer free, I am left with the health problems of a very optimistic septuagenarian. I lecture strangers about colonoscopies. I have mysterious ailments and random lumps that make people start sentences with "Well, at least . . ." And like every retiree, I accept ongoing and future pain as an unwanted assignment.

Sometimes suffering will make you better, so much better than you wanted to be. It has the wonderful advantage of sloughing off some of the soft rot in the human heart. Like ignorance. That is probably the first thing to go. Slice, slice. Then arrogance. Cut, cut. This is the forced humility of experience. It's hard to feel better than other people when you are certain that you are made up of sadness and deli meat.

Because suffering is mostly a knife, cutting away parts of you that, all things considered, you would prefer to keep *thankyouverymuch,* and when it ends—when you survey what's left—people will expect you to be filling your gratitude journal, while you feel like a coroner.

Hard to say it better than Job. We are "born unto trouble, as the sparks fly upward."

People who have suffered greatly—suffered unimaginably—will say that you never set your burdens down exactly. You learn how to carry them as you shoulder all the other invisible challenges that come with the imperceptible changes of becoming someone new. But I had sort of hoped that there was an unspoken guarantee that it would all get easier.

It didn't. Life went on and it became harder and harder to feel like it was the miracle everyone told me it was.

I have been explaining all this to my psychologist, Henry, who I started seeing when I was very sick. I report that I've been googling the symptoms for an anxiety disorder. "I feel buzzy," I say. "Like I'm alert but it's not useful . . ." He explains that what I have might not technically be a disorder if what I'm alert about (cancer! loss!) is concrete and likely imminent. How comforting. Perhaps it is the feeling that philosopher Martin Heidegger described about the moment people awaken to their own helplessness. This is the *thrownness* of life, Heidegger explained, the way we cannot choose our future. We drift between currents like helium balloons in the sky.

I know how today will go because it was the same feeling yesterday. I will feel like I was supposed to get to something—some list? some task? some relationship?—that gives me back a sense of fullness. *There, I did it*. But when I pile up every effort and attempt at completing something, it is only then that I can see the unfinishedness of it all. The poet Anne Sexton was right: "I am a collection of dismantled almosts."

Eventually I will notice the ridiculous wastefulness of all my efforts to be smarter, thinner, kinder, and entirely up to date on international affairs (and the latest season of *Love Island*). Sometime before bed I will have to reckon with the amount of time I spent finding wide shoes on the internet for the modern paddle-footed woman or trying to cycle off the thirteen pounds gained on last summer's camping trip from Hades. What I thought was progress was probably an imperceptible decline. The patron saint of the middle-aged woman, Nora Ephron, said of all this effort: "Maintenance is what they mean when they say, 'After a certain point, it's just patch patch patch.'"

I would gladly say any of this out loud, but I alternate between feeling embarrassed, justified, and like a closet narcissist. It feels like wanting more shouldn't be a question at all. A person who almost lost everything should know precisely the value of everything kept and everything lost. I should be too grateful to ask for more.

Except that no one tells you how fast it goes—the speed at which you can lay your own dreams down. After a diagnosis, a layoff, a divorce. A miscarriage, an accident, or an excruciating goodbye. You can lay the future down. You must.

Suffering is not a series of subtractions, it's a hurricane. And you thought you would spend your time doing the work of pain—that actual crisis of rupture and loss—but, no, it's mostly the salvaging and the paperwork and the difficult conversations about how everyone will (or probably won't) adjust to what's happened that takes you apart.

You're left there, looking at the rubble while everyone else's homes seem remarkably intact. In fact, the entire neighborhood looks perfectly new. Oh, wonderful, someone is powerwashing their driveway while someone else is walking their dog past you on the sidewalk. Here you are trying to pick up the scattered semblance of emotional, physical, and financial predictability off the lawn.

I always felt this in flashes, bursts of realization that the ordinariness of other people's concerns struck me as a betrayal.

I notice how quickly I judge other people for their obliviousness to pain, but then, wait.

It's Tuesday again.

My primary concern is email and that strange buzzy feeling in my head. And the guilt—oh, the guilt—of being so very busy worrying about nothing terribly important at all.

When I was dying, I believed that I would never forget the cost of survival and the surrender of the ordinary. An inalienable citizenship with all those who suffer was mine. And this awareness would quarry a reservoir of gratitude so deep that it could never be emptied. I was scarred, I was transformed, I was changed.

But not enough.

2

The Ache

I HAVE LONG BELIEVED the term *girls' weekend* should be replaced by the more accurate description *immersive therapy weekend* because of the exacting nature by which women can expertly take each other's problems apart in any location and concurrent with any activity. Upset about the low point of your relationship in the middle of a group salsa lesson? Tell me about how he never sent flowers for your grandmother's funeral, but give me a right turn, left turn, and a cross-body lead. That's female friendship.

Sometimes it will take the entire weekend to get through the bulk of it—the trading of stories, from the "Start from the beginning" to the tired satisfaction that we have wrung out every bit of meaning. *How did he say it again? Remember how your mom did the same thing to you before?* There is a truth carried through feminist thought that impresses itself upon me in these moments: women are split in two. There is a public self and a private one. The public self is chiseled out of every small moment in which a girl learns to be culturally "acceptable"—pliable, generous, erasable. You will think that you do not have a public self and you will play the part of a normal person with typical wants and needs (Starbucks! soft pants!). But then you will feel the need to close a door. Or pick up a phone. Or scream into the ocean as if you really, truly believed no one was listening. That feeling is the realization that sexism is the Greatest Show on Earth. We are sawed in half. Right there in public. Right before our very own eyes.

The Best Friend and I have already finished screen-printing, boozy brunching, massages, and something called "Contra Dancing," which is actually a country folk dance and not, as my father surmised, a festive assembly of Nicaraguan rebels from the 1980s. But now, after dance class and before dinner, I can sense some kind of intervention brewing because we have each been stuck in our own loops.

I have been stuck in the loop of chronic pain, interminable health appointments, work bureaucracy, and the same fight with my husband where we both play our parts with increasingly less creativity.

The sameness—the sameness—the sameness. Patch patch patch. It is a dark determinism.

Theologically speaking, I believe we have tremendous freedom to make meaningful choices each and every day. (A belief in predestination, in my humble opinion, tends to be wielded as a weapon by people who don't desperately need anything to change.) Unlike the charmingly cheerless Reformed folk who surround me at every turn, I do not believe in a hyper-causal universe where every step has already been laid out on the bed like an Easter dress.

So how is it possible that *every single day* of pushing reality uphill results only in it rolling back on me by nightfall?

I discovered the Best Friend's version of this feeling of being overwhelmed by the terrible sameness as we sat in her car outside of the restaurant on our last night together, the rain pouring down in sheets. She finally said it out loud.

"I can do this," she murmured in a low voice, and I strained to hear her over the din. "I can stay like this forever."

Like this.

Licking up these crumbs.

Making soup from these bones.

Feeling the human heart neatly poured into measuring cups.

All this want, and yet such determination: *Don't worry, don't worry, it's enough.*

For her, this was about *him*, obviously.

Even his name saved as a contact in her phone worried her.

They met when they were both substitute teachers at the same school and they stayed friends, year over year, which was fine. He was with someone and wasn't able to be hers anyway, but he called or texted something interesting or funny or remarkable every day (which could be mistaken for something concretely better than a relationship). Marriage, for instance, requires patience with someone who snores with the efficiency of an industrial meat grinder. Marriage asks you to really come to terms with what it's like to see him eat—I mean, really eat—and to decide that nothing you see stops you short. And what did it matter? She was good at every kind of love, and this love was friendship.

It took her about two years to admit that he was uniquely

beautiful, which he is. He has a Roman nose, sharp eyes, and is poured like concrete. Even better, he doesn't advertise his pheromones with a cloud of butterscotch cologne. He smells like clean laundry. When he thinks, his hand rubbing his chin, his stubble makes that satisfying scratchy sound. Hearing this, the Best Friend realized she was more wound up and more relaxed than she thought she could possibly be. He does that to her. She keeps thinking that she will meet someone else like him, pass his scent in the grocery store or start talking to someone on a conference call and feel that same static, but no. Only he has that particular combination of detergent and manic energy. The reality of him settled in her mind the more it went on. His voice, his sudden way of talking the instant she picks up the phone, even the sharp inhale he takes when he is about to make an argument—it all strikes her as unusual, almost annoyingly so. She can feel herself noticing these characteristics and trying to commit them to memory so that later she remembers what *he* did, what *he* would say about that, and she'll try to find reasons to bring these facts up casually in conversation like the weather and Wikipedia and the news.

He has written his signature all over everything. *This is mine. This is mine, too.*

When you are in the middle of a moment like this, you are probably the last to know. But everyone else knows. The fox knows. In a classic children's book set on a faraway planet, a fox meets the little prince and tells it like a warning: *For me you're only a little boy just like a hundred thousand other little boys. And I have no need of you.* But it will go the way it always goes: exchanges will build habits, habits expectations,

expectations ties, and these ties will tame them both. Then they will need each other.

"What is he for?" my friend started asking, sometime around year three. *What is all this for?*

"I guess it depends what kind of story this is," I would say, and we would repeat, again, that it can't be a love story. He was with someone else.

Now, in the car in the pouring rain, she wonders again, "So then what kind of story is this?"

Is this a gift or is this a warning?

"I don't know, hon. But I don't like that this seems to be hurting you."

"But I don't know if it's hurting me," she says absently, turning it over and over in her mind.

It is always night when we are frank about these matters, driving or stalking the streets of our neighborhoods miles away from each other, listening to each other breathe through the phone. Because if we were to stand still against the dark, we would hear the wind whistling through the slats of the shutters of the houses, pressing into the crevices of the foundations, announcing the cracks in everything.

We start calling it "the ache."

Sometimes it comes in a fleeting heartbreak. *He doesn't love me.* Other times it feels like carrying an anchor sewn into the lining of your stomach. *Will my body ever feel whole again?* And often it is just a persistent longing, which is never satisfied by a to-do list, a rushing from task to task, or the quick kiss and an automatic "Love you" before lights out. Sometimes the ache arrives as I watch a terrible movie about pirates and a throwaway line about a daughter being her father's true treasure strikes a certain sad note in me. Then, there it is. How ridiculous.

"Wait. Wasn't that pirate dad thing a scene in the fifth installment of *Pirates of the Caribbean: Dead Men Tell No Tales?*" the Best Friend asks.

"I need you to stop knowing things right now," I say flatly and move on.

Of course, the world will offer you no end of opportunities to mirror your own fears, childhood wounds, or unexpressed desires. Human beings, as it turns out, are not assembled from prefabricated parts and carefully constructed with an instruction manual close at hand. No, we are forged in the scrapyards of our parents' best and incomplete efforts and our own inevitable failures.

But the ache is not a feeling so much as a question. A question that starts with: "Will I . . . ?"

Will I ever feel completely known?

Will I ever feel like it's all enough?

Will I ever feel valued? Special. Supported. Less like a moron. Connected. Accomplished. Loved?

We might wish that any single emotion could map the whole terrain of that feeling—or at least tell us where to go—but nothing is quite like it.

The ache is durable in the same way that sadness—the heaviness of sadness—impresses itself upon you, making its demands. It is unrelenting in the same way that grief can be.

You can press your whole weight on the locked door of grief. You can scream and pound and try the lock again and again, and whatever your heart is wretched for will not open itself to you.

And in those moments when we feel certain that we'll die of longing, we don't.

It is an absence that drills a bitter well. We drink and drink and drink, hoping we can run it dry but more bubbles up from the deep. And still we thirst.

3

Things I Worry I Will Not Survive: An Incomplete List

1. Cancer. I mean, that makes sense.

2. Peaking in high school or worrying about peaking in high school. Since I sacrificed most of my twenties to the gods of academia and my thirties to illness, there wasn't a lot of time in there to feel, I don't know, attractive?

3. How useless I am in the face of global chaos.

4. Not having the relationships I need. Probably the greatest casualty of having multiple health problems isn't money, it's friends.

5. The desire to look carefree on social media. Bring back the filters. For the love of all that is blanched, bring them back.

6. The length of pharmaceutical ads on what's left of cable television. May cause unintended diagnosis and undue

phone calls to people who admitted at a party that they work in a hospital setting. False negatives may occur.

7. The death of my dad, who glues something together. Man after my own historical heart. Sarcasm of my soul.

8. The ache.

4

Hungry, Hungry Hippos

My sisters and I used to crowd around the red plastic game board of Hungry Hungry Hippos pounding the black handles with our fists. We added marbles and more marbles so that the tray was swimming with them. Our hippos—mine named Henry—opened their mouths to swallow as many as possible, as fast as possible. We screamed. We pushed each other off. We always wanted more.

These days, I look around and all I see are hungry, hungry hippos. We want and we want and we want. If we were making Christmas lists, we would only write, *More!*

The Portuguese have a wonderful word, which like all wonderful words from other languages can't be translated exactly. The term is *saudade*. It means "a somewhat melancholic feeling of incompleteness" or "an indolent dreaming wistfulness" or "the memory of things lost" or "a pleasure you suffer, an ailment you enjoy." In musical form, *saudade* infuses a style called *fado*. In fact, most cultures have a music centered on longing—Americans have the blues, Japanese have *enka;* it's *flamenco* in Spanish, *rebetiko* in Greek, and *ghazals* in Urdu. Around the globe right now, there are people hunched over a guitar, a bouzouki, or a harmonium singing about what they want but somehow can never have.

We flutter without landing. And that's the way it's always been. Even in the fourth century Saint Augustine spoke of this perpetual yearning as being innate in everyone. The writer Glennon Doyle beautifully described the ache as a deep and ferocious call from inside and outside of herself which she experienced as an inescapable force of "lovepainbeautytendernesslonginggoodbye." Perhaps if we reached for a single word for it, we might turn to the German playwright Friedrich Schiller who called it *Sehnsucht:* a deep, bittersweet longing—often for something lost or never fully possessed, like a spiritual home. That's who we are; humans are the species with a hole inside us.

The Stoic philosopher Seneca considered this kind of feeling a curse, saying that "though you possess the world, you will yet be miserable."

But who do I know who feels like they possess the world? Don't we always feel a gap in our lives? At this moment aren't we all missing someone, managing a loss, or struggling to achieve something just beyond our grasp? Someone at the peak of their potential has been laid off from their job. A young family suffers a miscarriage. A grandmother sees her children and grandchildren moving far away. A single mother is acting as teacher and physical therapist and caregiver to her child with special needs. Who hasn't wondered whether they were ever going to find that sense of purpose that should give meaning to their life?

This ache may not dominate our existence; we carry on—of course we do—and succeed sometimes, we enjoy pleasurable moments with our friends, find nourishment in poignant memories, but there always remains a strange restlessness in us that can't be snuffed out. Fulfillment is too fleeting and we are bothered by the realization that *maybe these are the good old days*.

Modernity tells us that we have infinite choices, that progress is mandatory, and that we have the power to make ourselves into something sparkling. But we know that's not true. If the universe has our back, why do I wake up in the morning with a pain in my lumbar region?

No self-help manual, no scheduling software, yoga class, or vision board, no hours of manifesting, self-medicating, or assertion training will ever fix us. No matter how we visualize our day, curb our emotions, or strive toward our "best life now," we cannot overcome the problem of finitude. We are never enough for ourselves and we always want more.

This is doubly painful because we feel ashamed of our inability to feel grateful. This guilt, argued Kierkegaard, only spirals into self-hatred for all the ways that we often undermine our own chances to live a good life.

We are, as the poet Goethe described, a "troubled guest on the dark earth."

5

The Basement

THE MOST UNFORGIVABLE things will happen to you. What happens, *happens*. And there will be no apology.

This was a truth that was passed down in my family like bone china.

Sometimes it was a story told by my nana, who set sail to Canada at the age of fourteen to hunt down the father who had abandoned her in search of Yukon gold, only to discover he had drowned in the Mackenzie River as a drunk and a fool.

Other times it is the best guess why the melodic abomination of Mannheim Steamroller found its way into the Christmas traditions of families the world over.

But I remember it most as a reason handed to me to explain my father.

It was as if someone had said, simply, every house has a basement. This man has a basement.

It began when I was very young, the way he would find the

quiet and the dark, and stay there. When he was not reading or sitting at the computer, he was sleeping or napping or dozing, and each state of these required a kind of silence that dampened every room. The phone would ring. A friend might want to stop by. The first few lines of another argument might break out among us. But nothing could last because *Your father is sleeping.*

My mother might have said: *Your father is deeply disappointed with his life.* A psychologist might have observed: *Your father is clinically depressed.* And a priest would have known that the soul forgets its own immeasurable worth.

Underneath every attempt at building a life and career and relationships lies another layer. And there, every kind of hidden thing can do its own work. Carl Jung called this the shadow side, "the thing a person has no wish to be." And this shadow impressed itself upon my father, so much so that the landscape of his life—an airport gate, a grocery store line, a friend's kitchen—would paint itself in grays and blacks. Later, much later, he would say that almost nothing about his midlife years rises to memory except the glimmers of his girls growing, shrieking, singing, rousing him from the dark.

This is the way I came to understand the feeling of ache and the sense that we are all strangers from one another—that all of us live inside of struggles that no one can entirely understand.

Some people get iron in their souls. That's how the author Thomas Hardy characterized it. A deposit of iron. And it pulls us *down, down, down.*

When I took my first psychology class in college, I was very interested to learn that people who study happiness have a basic theory about "set points." The theory is that half of your happiness (or sadness) is hardwired. Your levels of satisfaction with your life won't go up or down much regardless of whether you win the lottery or suffer a tragic accident. You will likely return to your baseline happiness level.

It all sounds very reasonable. Except if your set point pulls you into the basement.

If you ever wondered whether it requires herculean efforts for some people to live each day, I would sing you a ridiculous song. It was the 1990s and even Canadians were in the throes of Jerry Springer, where the shouts of "Jerry! Jerry! Jerry!" would reveal the results of yet another paternity test. So that chant started as something of a joke in my house, which became a refrain, which can still bring tears to my eyes.

The house would be utterly still except the sound of my father snoring down the hall. My mom and two sisters—so many little women—would tiptoe around, washing and putting away dishes quietly, arguing over homework or clothes or who called dibs on the hallway phone. We became fragile and resentful in the dark with his absence and presence all around us. But with my homework on the kitchen table, the light scribbling of my pen in an open notebook, I could almost always hear it. He had a song for everything: crossing the street quickly, showering in a hurry, and a very annoying use of hand trumpets to wake me up in the morning. But this was my favorite—the soft daily cheer of his own name.

"Jerry! Jerry! Jerry!"

Which meant, today, he would get up. He would pop his

head out of his soul's basement. He would try again. Sometimes, the beauty of watching someone *try* is astonishing.

But for the most part, the house remained quiet and all of us scuttled around in the dark. What happens, *happened*. And there would be no apology.

6

I Asked Strangers on the Internet What They Ache For: A List

1. "One more moment with my son."

2. "Some peace of mind about money would be nice. Send me some?"

3. "Somewhere to call home."

4. "For my soulmate to live forever. Yes, I'm talking about my dog."

5. "Being pain free for a day."

6. "A real friend who returns your text right away and doesn't make you feel weird when you ask for something."

7. "A cure for regret. And an explanation for why I still want him back."

8. "Allergy relief, for the love of all that is pollen."

9. "My daughter-in-law to stop trash-talking me to my son."

10. "A job that makes my family respect me."

11. "Potato chips."

7
―

Ashes Than Dust

I LIVE IN A country whose foundational myths are about having it all. Health. Wealth. Happiness. And I have made studying those myths my life's work.

I say "myths" not because I am trying to imply that these stories are false, even though it is actually impossible for an entire country with millions of people to each have it *all*. A few people will have a lot and a lot more people will have almost nothing. But a myth is a perfect way to describe a story that has been repeated so many times and in so many different ways that it feels universal, true—sacred even.

In the late nineteenth century, the most popular myths were those that explained how to navigate the deep unfairness of life. Who could survive the hustle and claw of an American Dream? What kind of striver—what kind of believer?—can climb the ladder from adversity to prosperity?

There are many philosophical, religious, economic, and

political valences to the answers, but the basic premise is this: *anything is possible for those who believe.*

No economic obstacle will limit a believer's prosperity. No negative thinking will obstruct their dreaming. Seek to devour the whole world and you will never go hungry.

This is why Americans think that they can solve the ache.
Everything is here.
Reach out and take it.
You simply haven't grasped hard enough.

I was going to say as much in my lecture to some very nice people at a fundraiser somewhere in California. The hotel was full of people giving money to an organization to end human trafficking, and I planned to say something deeply wise about the failures of the prosperity gospel sometime around dinner. But it was breakfast and I had a lot of time to kill.

I looked around the table full of people eating scrambled eggs and toast and slimy honeydew melon and saw only one person who was not caught up in a conversation. In fact, he looked paralyzingly bored.

"Heyyyyyyyyy!" I said, half whispering across the table so as not to disturb the other guests. "Hey!"

He looked up, slightly alarmed.

"Yes! You! Hello," I said and paused.

He simply stared at me through his dark-rimmed glasses. I vaguely recognized him from the opening-night party the evening prior.

"Look, I have a rental car," I went on.

I didn't realize how ridiculous this sounded until I heard myself speak the sentence out loud. *Hello, stranger. Will you come with me in my rental vehicle? I have candy in my windowless van!* But I was only warming up. I pulled my phone out of my purse and clicked on my favorite app: Roadside America. It contains a map of the United States and Canada with markers for every local attraction and colorful descriptions luring you to visit.

"There's a couple things to see around here . . . I'm probably going to visit, um, well, it says that there are some bear boots from 1851. These boots are actually bear legs, dehydrated bear legs . . . oh geez. The claws and everything. Um . . . future Civil War General Joseph Hooker fought the bear with his . . . hands. And now people can wear the . . . legs."

I looked up and saw that the man's facial expression had not changed. But I knew in my heart that I was going to see the bear legs with or without him.

"Okay, well that's not all. There's a bathtub on stilts . . . Only an hour away. Noah's Ark, but honestly I've already seen the giant Noah's Ark in Kentucky with my dad. Okay, how about this? There's a state park and a graveyard about forty-five minutes away."

Then he spoke, at last.

"I'll meet you in the parking lot," he said, putting on his blazer.

We drove about an hour outside of town and parked at a small, clearly marked trailhead. Soon we were walking side by side down a winding forest trail. The earth was damp and the path soft underfoot, and the towering groves of redwoods and bigleaf maples were enough to make us believe that this was the right sort of staging ground for a pretty majestic bear fight, if it came to that.

My adventuring companion was already turning out to be an unusual sort of person. He had been more interested than anyone *has ever been* in listening to the stories of my travels to see the world's largest Noah's Ark in Kentucky. But I had to stop walking and gape for a minute when I discovered that he had gone on a journey to a similar biblical re-creation in rural Alberta. And, lo and behold, he was also a historian obsessed with mythmaking. His name was Tom Holland—not Tom Holland the actor. In fact, that was pretty much how it went every time I heard him introduced from then on. "His name is Tom Holland, not the actor who played Spider-Man." But famous nonetheless with a wonderful history podcast and plenty of bestselling books, but most important, he was not the kind of stranger to murder me in the woods.

It turns out that his long silence at the breakfast table had probably been some kind of confusion over the fact that anyone else on the planet would want to leave a nice hotel to drive out to the middle of the woods and think about history. But there I was.

By that time a friendly park warden whizzed by in a golf cart and noticed that we were wearing entirely the wrong shoes. He said he was happy to pick us up and we gratefully climbed in beside him. With much seriousness, he explained the significance of the site along the way.

The park had been named after the author Jack London who built his enormous dream home there in the forest. Jack had been one of the world's most famous writers and adventurers, known for his almost two hundred books and short stories—like *White Fang* and *The Call of the Wild*. But it was the man himself who inspired the legend. Jack had been stranded, imprisoned, homeless, and adrift at sea; a whaler, gold prospector, war correspondent, coal shoveler, and, finally, a rancher. He had fallen in love with a woman named Charmian, who was every bit as wild as Jack. He built them a two-masted ketch called *The Snark* with plans to sail around the world together. After they fell ill from tropical diseases they picked up on the voyage, they moved out to these woods to build the multi-floor stone mansion of their dreams where they planned to live out their days innovating as farmers and ranchers. At least that's what Tom and I learned before we were summarily dumped out of the ranger's golf cart at Jack and Charmian's gravesite.

We stood and stared at the burial site for a good long time. Here Jack and Charmian lay together in the ruins of the home they built.

"This is a pretty tip-top grave," said Tom Holland (not the actor) contemplatively.

It was. Jack and Charmian had scratched every itch, lived out every adventure, and gone to the edges of the earth to embody every dream. Even thinking about it I could feel the great engine at the heart of every American story about want: you are on a great journey to have everything. *Go, go, go.*

The nearby museum devoted to Jack and Charmian was lovely and informative, with Jack's powerful philosophy emblazoned on the wall:

I would rather be ashes than dust!
I would rather that my spark should burn out in a brilliant blaze than it should be stifled by dry-rot.
I would rather be a superb meteor, every atom of me in magnificent glow,
than a sleepy and permanent planet.
The purpose of man is to live, not to exist.
I shall not waste my days in trying to prolong them.
I shall use my time.

It was beautiful. It was breathless with inspiration.

And I was immediately livid.

"Well, that's very nice," I said to no one in particular because Tom had already wandered off to another part of the exhibit. "It says here in his biography that when he got together with Charmian he *already had a wife and two children.* Who is taking care of his kids while he's traipsing around the world eating pineapples with a new wife?"

Something about the photograph of Jack in his bathing costume among the palm trees of Hawaii set me off. That man was having the time of his life. And eating pineapples.

"His new wife seems to have been a really formidable woman," observed Tom, back again and looking up at the photographs of the two of them laughing. I frowned. She had been quite the adventurer, I could give her that much, and she was devoted to him for what little time he had. He died at age forty of mercury poisoning from all the excesses of alcohol and devouring raw duck, entirely worn through from having lived life to its fullest.

Playwright George Bernard Shaw probably would have approved. "I want to be thoroughly used up when I die, for the harder I work, the more I live. I rejoice in life for its own sake. Life is no 'brief candle' for me. It is a sort of splendid torch, which I have got hold of for the moment." Shaw baptized the hard work of living as downright sacred.

"This entire thing really bothers me," I told Tom, who was appropriately enraptured by having discovered a historical treasure in the middle of the day. But it wasn't until long after we left and drove back to the hotel, only when I was standing up to give my lecture, that I could feel the pieces of my anger falling into place.

"It is a common American myth about happiness that everything you need is already there for the taking," I said, pacing and staring at the floor. "And maybe it is."

Perhaps you can leave home. Perhaps you can sail around the world. Maybe there is more, more, more. Jack London devoured the whole world. He used his time in exactly the way he wanted.

Does the *go, go, go* solve the ache inside of us?

"It seems to me that an enormous part of the American Dream is the promise of totalizing happiness. That the more you want, the more you shall have. There are no limits in a world of *everything is possible*."

But at what cost? What about the obligations, the loves, the choices that bind?

Men like Jack London can devour the whole world, and history loves them despite each moment of selfishness that took them away from quieter loves, good anonymous responsibilities—like two young daughters who barely knew their father and the first wife who had to stay home to raise them. But there is no universe in which a good *woman* leaves. A good man can buy fame and adventure and love. A good woman will inevitably lose as much as she gains.

The myth stands: you are on a great journey and you ache for more. *Go, go, go.*

But if you ache, will you lose it all? *Stay, stay, stay.* Sometimes there are too many errands and doctor's appointments to go searching. Not even in our own backyards. I am needed. I am busy. I have good things to attend to.

Saint Augustine knew it was not either-or. "I am but dust *and* ashes," he wrote. Abraham said as much. So did Job.

Sometimes we must stay where we are. But there will be a question that bubbles up from the deep. A question that must be asked and answered in some form or another. What is the cost of going? I look at a man eating pineapples and think, *obvious.* Of course. Some people pretend they have no obligations.

But who will stand over the rest of us when we are dust and know the true cost of the fact that we stayed?

8

The House

PEOPLE WILL WALK you through their lives like a series of rooms.

It is an image that is both ancient and divine. Our souls are like castles, observed Saint Teresa of Ávila, containing many rooms. And in the very center is God.

But usually it sounds more like:

Welcome! Don't mind my mom hovering in the kitchen. Yes, that's where Grandpa sleeps on the chair we've been trying to take to the dump since 1987. The mold issue in the basement is absolutely without a doubt the reason my sister has asthma, but we are committed to gaslighting her about having allergies. All the couches are dark to absorb stains because we usually end up eating in front of the television and the most important feature is the lock on the bathroom door so—for the love of all that is holy—I can be alone for once.

We are surrounded by all the evidence of every choice we have ever made—the sofa, the wedding china, that relationship to the adult man playing Xbox. And every choice that was handed to us as our inheritance—those in-laws, these freckles, his high school poster collection with a dog on a motorcycle that reads REBEL WITHOUT A BONE. There is a great word for what happens when we live intertwined lives: *quiddity*. It means the peculiarity, the essence of someone, the thing that makes them one thing and not another. Taken together, we see all the weird and wonderful specificity of the "whatness" of it all.

Each room quiets. As my favorite poet-mortician Thomas Lynch describes, "the room, once you vacated it, returned to stone and fire and a chair and the old ghosts." Animism in reverse.

The most obvious features of our lives are the walls. Poured in concrete. Lined with photographs.

We accumulate so many loves and responsibilities and obligations that we need weight-bearing structures to shelter them in place. A kid. Another kid. Parents. Friends. Dependents in all directions. Find me a human without burdens and I will point out that you are gesturing to a newborn baby still dewy from birth. Or someone yelling "Woooooooo!" on spring break.

Still, we are desperate to become the kind of people who can shoulder it all.

We want to be the daughter or son who nods and smiles at every overtold story.

The parent who does not resent the seemingly weekly school bake sale.

The partner who doesn't need to use the calendar to figure out how old you are again.

The friend who is comfortable offering psychological assessments about your ex-boyfriend. (*Definitely a narcissist. Don't look it up. We don't need to, babe.*)

We want to carry it all with love, with grace.

I have a perfect friend who is built like a boxcar and lifts weights like someone preparing to put forklifts out of business. He does this because he has a daughter who had a brain tumor and now she can't get out of bed without him and he needs to lift her, turn her, carry her, as long as he can. So he will, because he is her load-bearer.

There are always loads to be carried.

We know this truth most when we have babies and they hang off of us, drape themselves over us, need us in a way that leaches the color from our hair and the sanity from our souls. Farewell, hygiene. So long, privacy. This is the price we pay for their creation and sustenance and the joys that burst out of their connection with us.

I was drinking coffee and staring out the window on a bleary morning and my son, six years old at the time, stumbled out of his room in dinosaur pajamas. He lurched over to me, sleepy and silent, climbing onto me and lying across my lap with most of his upper body dangling upside down over the edge of the chair.

"Mum," he said, eyes closed. "Do you think you really felt *prepared* for parenthood?"

Before I could reply, he added, "And can I have a Band-Aid?"

"Why?"

He opened one eye and gauged my reaction. "It's two bites," he said, and closed his eyes.

I jolted to attention and started pulling up his shirt. Nothing on his stomach.

"What bit you?" I asked as evenly as possible, tugging up a pant leg.

"Salamanders," he sighed, still upside down, and raised both index fingers. "Two different ones. Veeeeeeery different personalities."

Look around and we will realize how much we shelter. Immovable health problems. Financial drains. Pets we didn't know we had.

And are we ever *really* prepared for parenthood?

Look again and see how we are sheltered by others' walls. We are propped up by every hug, check-in, errand, and plastic container of soup sitting in our freezers that a lady from book club cooked up for our convenience or emergency. Sometimes we are not so much born as built.

"I found the joystick for the Apple IIc," said my father on the phone this week, referring to an accessory for a 1984 Macintosh computer on which we had learned about the early horrors of the Oregon Trail. My father doesn't say "Hello" or "How are you?" Just: "I went looking for a USB cable and I found forty, if you need any. I won't throw them out in case you need one."

At some point, probably around the thirtieth USB cable, we should all stop to look around with a growing concern. I mean, really, whose house is this? I never found the salamanders.

I chose this. And I didn't.

I want to fill my life with more. More happiness, more contentment, maybe some vacation time without my laptop. But sometimes all I can see are walls. The bills I need to pay. The people I have chosen to love. The body I have that won't cooperate.

There's so much that's just not possible because, well, life.

Sometimes we feel like we might burst because it is all so much—too much—and yet never enough.

It is a truth that medieval philosophy summarized with the dictum "Every choice is a renunciation . . . To choose one thing is to turn one's back on many others." We truly cannot have everything. Or even *most* things?

So I try to tuck away honest resentments like a quilt folded in the hallway closet.

These rooms are too full and too empty.

But we can't say that, of course.

9

What Causes the Ache: An Incomplete List

1. The baby you didn't have.
2. Fear for the ones you did.
3. Thinking too carefully about the future of polar bears and bees.
4. What's going on with any ex, anywhere.
5. He's not happier, is he? Gosh, I hope not.
6. Floating unknown in a sea of email.
7. Parents gone too soon.
8. Losing parents before death anyway.
9. Realizing not everything is going to "fall into place."
10. Concern that you waited too long.
11. The chronic problem that never goes away.

12. Not seeing the pyramids.

13. Seeing the pyramids but looking back and realizing you were too stressed about everything to enjoy them, for Pete's sake.

14. Realizing you're the kind of person who misses out on life because you are too busy taking care of other people, falling into the quicksand of pain, or discounting your nicest moments.

15. Everyone knows it.

10

Toxic Positivity

I WANT TO TELL everyone I've ever met—*I'm happy! I'm happy with the life I have!* A woman like that is never robbed by past regrets. Or stirred by future fears. She is shockingly buoyed by forces visible and invisible. Hers is a fitless peace. She always eats what's on the menu.

A woman like that is completely enamored with the job of her dreams. A life in academia is its own kind of hallucinogenic experience: a maze of buildings quarried from similar stone, the sudden appearance of a school mascot with a confusing sense of moral superiority, and a set of vending machines for a late-night Coke Zero. Duke University has been my favorite of them all. When the writer Aldous Huxley walked around the campus, he declared that it was "the most successful essay in neo-Gothic that I know," which really means that, if I'm a decent shot, I could throw a rock in any direction and hit an arch, parapet, gargoyle, or all three.

I was *almost* young here, or at least that's how it feels. I was hired as a professor at twenty-eight, but because I teach in the master's and doctoral programs, my students were my same age and we all had to pretend I was much older. So I did what any significantly-less-attractive Elle Woods would do: I adopted the scholarly uniform of a houndstooth blazer with elbow patches and reading glasses, despite the fact that my eyes are two of the only non-compromised organs I have. Then when the glasses gave me a headache I was back to the full flower of my New Girl stage where I was unsuccessfully being walked around the earth by an enormous set of bangs.

But the moment I get out of the car and see (with my fantastic vision) the sight of the chapel reaching into the cloudy sky, I feel like I am in the center of the world again. My usual classroom sits at the bottom of a sprawling staircase in the main building of the divinity school. There in those familiar walls I have taught some version of a Toxic Positivity class for about twenty years and it is a huge bummer. Elite universities have a long-standing obsession with trying to teach their students to be happy, which has its uses. Of course we want everyone to be happy. Of course we want students to have good mental health. But I like to argue that there are downsides to being up, so I do.

"Hello, lovelies," I say, pulling up my lecture on my iPad and setting it on the lectern. "Let's begin. America is a nation of incurable optimists. *Good vibes only. Don't worry, be happy. Look on the bright side. A positive mindset is everything.* Yes, the past is littered with mistakes, but the future will march on to the steady drumbeat of self-improvement. How many of you think that America is the happiest country on earth?"

Most of the hands go up, though some are paused midair, looking around to see what others have decided.

"Good job to all those of you who sensed that this question was a trap. But let's agree that America is in the top fifty of the happiest countries. Hands up?"

All the hands go up again.

"Ha hahhhhhh! Guys! You know I'm using my evil voice! It's obviously a trap. But don't worry. There are one hundred and forty countries ranked in the annual World Happiness Report. And America is in the top forty percent."

There are some murmurs and smiles and the students are ready to move on.

"I AM OBVIOUSLY LYING TO YOU!" I continue at an unhelpful volume. "The United States is an unhappier country every year! If you're under thirty, America is not even in the top sixty of the world's most content nations. The country is rife with glaring racial, social, and economic inequality that makes huge swaths of the population miserable. But still this unhappy America is a cult of positivity. *Just believe! Success will follow! Optimism itself will save us.* Americans believe in positivity—no matter whether the stock market is soaring or falling or how many people are suffering."

It's already a wonderfully depressing start to the lecture but my students have decided to keep their hands and heads down to take notes so I can't see the light go out of their eyes. Every semester I explain how America became a country of bright-siders and why optimism can be a dangerous obsession. I try not to say "dangerous obsession" in an ominous voice because it's an academic analysis, but that's the gist. Dating back to the success manuals sold in the heart of America's first big cities, the marketplace has been flooded with a century of products and celebrities promising the secrets to happiness. From multilevel marketing schemes and televangelism to business gurus and Peloton, modern positivity is now a multi-billion-dollar industry, a massive enterprise developed over the twentieth century, preying on the insecurities of all those who can't achieve the American Dream.

Our culture of happiness has strict social rules, which makes expressing negative emotions unacceptable. People feel pressure to bypass sadness, frustration, and despair altogether. Or, at the very least, these emotions are usually masked in public. Whether it is bypassing or masking, many of us believe in the gospel of *Fake It 'Til You Make It*.

Sometimes outsiders notice this, like Alexander Schmemann did. A priest from Estonia, he was a keen observer of American psychology. "A certain image of America," he wrote in his diary, is this kind of relentless "keep smiling." But he thought it was a "superficial harmony" that could break down when it becomes clear there's no room for either grief or joy in such a world.

Instead, we ought to be listening to the psychologist Lisa Damour, who offers a wonderfully reassuring definition of mental health that has absolutely nothing to do with being consistently happy. Mental health, she argues, is actually about feeling what is appropriate to the situation. In a traffic accident? Fear and anger sound right. Thinking about your friend who went through cancer with you? Sadness is key. When we allow ourselves to experience the whole range of human emotion, there can be no "wrong" emotion. Who knows? We might even spare ourselves secondary pain—that unnecessary suffering born of the guilt and shame of not looking on the bright side of life.

There is something very satisfying about giving this kind of lecture to people who will go on to lead churches and communities, because maybe they will help people to stop pretending to be happy, when it seems so central to the American way of being. America hums with the obsessive belief that there is a cure for every want. Decade after decade roils with new promises, new solutions, new prophets of good, better, best. We live on the scorched earth of every failed revival promising to solve for pain through the sweetness of our efforts.

It's January, and I know that by the end of the semester, students will be wonderfully deflated. Anyone who accidentally came into class with a RADIATE POSITIVITY sticker on her water bottle will tuck that in her bag. The one girl in a ponytail in the front row will stop wearing her NO BAD DAYS sweatshirt.

Soon they will know that the terrible genius of "toxic positivity" is that it actually *makes us sad*. We cannot be honest. We cannot develop genuine resilience because we cannot name what we have lost. And, worst of all, this kind of optimism prevents us from imagining social and structural solutions to the problems that keep us hooked on positivity in the first place.

I believe every word that I will say this semester. It took me a decade to finish an exhaustive history about positive thinking with painstaking archival research and hundreds of interviews with leaders and believers alike.

And yet.

There is a kind of more-than-enoughness that I long for. It is deep. It touches the soul. And I have no idea how to satisfy my heart's true desires. I'm too busy right now, actually.

I would try to become happier, but I've got an overflowing inbox, school pickups, physical therapy, faculty meetings, and this class to teach.

11

The Formula That Solves Everything

ONE NIGHT AT dinner, I really understood that the ache wasn't going anywhere.

Traffic had been bad and the dining room in the restaurant was too warm, and we all said so while we were being seated, even though one of the rules for our gathering was No Small Talk. So that died down immediately when the moderator cleared her throat. The eight of us sat a little taller in our chairs for a second, as if called to attention.

I laughed quietly to myself. *What was I doing here?* I had been invited by a friend (who had been invited by his friend) to this Washington, D.C., restaurant but the whole thing seemed to operate like one of those chain letters I received as a child. "Do this (top secret!), but send it along to three friends." By the time I had agreed to come to the dinner, however, the original friend couldn't make it and I was conscripted into the hands of strangers with a firm set of instructions about the premise of this evening: a chance for a one-time, one-shot conversation with randoms who, like you, knew the rules. No small talk. No speeches. No last names. And, my personal favorite: No being boring. We would simply eat a meal together, someone would be appointed moderator to keep things moving, and we would stick to a series of meaningful topics with the kind of intellectual focus and emotional vulnerability typically reserved for, well, no one. How often do we sit down and hammer out our answers to existential questions that keep pulling at the threads of our minds at 2:00 A.M.?

The clink and the clatter from the nearby kitchen had a settling effect on us, and introductions were traded as we passed around a petite sirah that the athletic man beside me in a puffy vest described as a "sleep inhibitor" until he got a sharp look from across the table. Oops. Points off for being boring. I liked this group already.

"I'd love to begin, if you'll let me," said a different man, his slender arms leaning into the table. "I wonder if you'd like to do a thought exercise with me." I looked around and everyone was nodding, and the moderator, a woman who reminded me of a young Elvira, Mistress of the Dark—if Elvira, Mistress of the Dark had gone into finance and wore a lot of structured blazers—gave a wave as if to say, proceed.

"I have come to my own conclusions," the man said gravely, "and, you'll have to be willing to agree or disagree to a set of statements by raising your hand." Well, this was already becoming a little bit too much "Play my little game," and I looked the questioner over more carefully until I understood the source of his confidence. He was in the news . . . a lot . . . one of those rare business owners whose success had created a permanent aura about him—but what had he done? I couldn't place it. Staring at him in dim light over a floral centerpiece, he looked youngish. Middle age had not yet decided whether to chew him up; he seemed lean and hungry as a puma. I had a fleeting concern that I would be asked to join an investment scheme (or death pact) with dessert.

"Do you need to change something about your life?"

Easy. All hands went up. There was a light chuckle of relief as we glanced around at one another. Next.

"Who here is happy?"

I started to raise my right hand and then stopped abruptly.

Am I really happy?

What is the purpose of my life?

Is my happiness something that can be improved?

Maybe people discuss this type of thing with their therapists. Maybe they scribble their answers in a journal kept in a drawer in the bedside table. But I worry that if I asked myself, openly, the questions that are so deeply necessary—if I really tried to address them—the answers would take my life apart.

I looked around. It turns out that none of us had moved quickly enough, and there was that small bit of laughter again as we saw how many of us were locked in a kind of midair wave.

"Yes or no?" said the puma, and I liked him less. I mean, he hadn't smiled once. Was *he* happy? And who can be happy *all the time*?

We all put our hands down, one by one, and brows furrowed because we had reasons. We all had reasons.

"Can we ask what you mean by happiness?" interrupted a voice. It was the man next to me, who had leaned both his cane and umbrella heavily on the table between our chairs. I had known instantly that he was a professor, because herringbone paired with sensible black running shoes is a staple of our kind, but I would find out later that he was a climate expert and he didn't like to throw around predictions.

"Just answer the question as best you can and we can debate the definitions in a moment," the puma replied. And the moderator sat there picking her long black nails.

"Last question. You said you want to change. You said you are unhappy. So consider this: if I told you there was a formula that could guarantee your complete emotional, mental, physical, and spiritual health, would you follow the formula?"

The waiter appeared at just that moment with his arms full of plates, and I could feel the collective exhale. We had hesitated, that much was clear. We were being told that there might be a Holy Grail of Life Satisfaction and we had hesitated.

Maybe we were skeptics and didn't like the premise.

Maybe we were realists and didn't see the usefulness of that kind of optimism.

Or maybe we were still busy sifting through all the evidence in our own lives. The idea that there is a formula for happiness appeals to every person who has wondered, deep down, if there is a secret to life. Do you have to be rich? Do you have to be a special kind of person? Is there a kind of completeness I have overlooked?

The puma was looking at us evenly, with the kind of unfazed general interest that indicated he had played this game before and would be bored by our answers. We were quiet, each lost to ourselves.

The moderator perked up then and pressed her manicured

hands together, about to break the silence, when the climate scientist cleared his throat.

"I've spent years leading research trips to the Arctic. You probably think you know the severity of glacial melt, but you don't . . ." He shook his head and trailed off, as if unsure that he had the energy to begin a speech he knew by heart.

The table was still, as if pooling strength for him, which the scientist seemed to appreciate. He pressed on.

"Did you know that we would rather poison ourselves?" he asked with an arched eyebrow. "I mean, really. That's not an exaggeration. We have enough information now, at this very moment, to make new policies that could reverse course on decades of environmental pollution, but no, we would rather be poisoned." Then he smacked the table loudly. The diner at a nearby table glanced toward us.

"We would rather satiate ourselves with trinkets and claw at one another for power than *save ourselves when we have the chance.*" The scientist's voice trembled as he raised his liver-spotted hand.

And we paused for a moment to consider this dramatic proclamation, but it was the loneliness that seemed to pour out of him that made me want to reach out and put a hand on his shoulder.

"Yeah, of course, I would take it," the puffy vest said at full volume, startling everyone. "The formula, I mean. I used to be a surfer and now I own a company focused on health wearables." He noticed some looks of light confusion. "You might have noticed the biowearables that can monitor glucose levels for diabetics, but this is a whole line of consumer goods that can translate the science of your body into usable data. So,

I'm always interested in reaching my maximum potential. An algorithm sounds attractive." And he put his hand up, and the puma nodded.

Other people started listing their worries and putting their hands up. They wanted out of the feeling of malaise. The not-being-sure what really matters. The burnout and overwhelm and sense that every effort is half-baked from the start.

"I'm not really supposed to be adding my own opinions," the moderator chimed in, smoothing her long hair down in front of her shoulder nervously. "But . . . I want the formula. I've, uh, had to make a lot of hard decisions lately so I could be there for my mom. She has early onset dementia, and it's been, well, it's not the kind of thing that people like hearing about. So yeah. Tell me the formula."

The puma sat back, and though his face changed very little, his eyes darted around with hawkish attentiveness before they landed on me. I didn't want to answer, I really didn't want to, because I don't believe. I don't believe in lambasting yourself for failing to be perfect and endless quests for the cure for being human. But still. Looking around. Wasn't there a feeling like lead that sat in the middle of my chest sometimes?

That there should be more, and that I haven't found it.

I put my hand up without comment. Consensus. And the puma smiled at last.

12

Fantastic Ideas I've Already Tried to Solve the Ache

1. Instagram accounts. I fixed myself with a click-bait hole and a $750 online course. The monthly challenges to revolutionize my life can be summarized by the phrases: drink water, be grateful, count your breaths. (Bonus: The air came free!)

2. Water bottles. Glamorous, two-handed, and impossible-to-fit-in-a-cup-holder water bottles. Apparently if I do not consume the weight of a fully matured female rhinoceros every day in ounces of water, I will perish. Pay no attention to the fact that I have never died before.

3. Compliments. Having gone to school for an extra decade to improve and refine my scholarship and my thinking, I want compliments. An endless stream of compliments. Was that so insightful? Thank you. But just wait until I walk you through the footnotes!

4. Spas. The great promise of wearing a white terry-towel robe in a soothing environment complete with cucumber-water stations is the hope that I will somehow become significantly more attractive by the time I leave.

5. Parenthood. I am raising a son who makes me feel like the clock of the universe was set by his birth. And now that should solve pretty much anything. I don't lie in the bath for hours having feelings other than totalizing satisfaction, no. That's never happened because I read all seventeen thousand emails I get from the school, and I cherish each and every holiday concert, even when one of the leads tried a British accent.

6. Jesus. The greatest source of love I know. Savior of the world, great bringer of truth, truly God, and present since the foundations of the earth were laid. Reeeeaaaallly not a solution to the problem of pain, sorry. When I get to heaven (fingers crossed!), I have a few suggestions I'd like to workshop.

13

The Algorithm

THE MEMORY OF the dinner lingered, and the species of man it uncovered. Men in puffy vests. Men with algorithms. Men with company logos. They stand astride the world—and soon, wherever it is their rockets will take them.

There is something so alien about an entire class of people who don't think of themselves as crawling through the tar pits of everyday suffering. Geniuses! These are winners, wellness elites with an appetite for measurable gains. An entire field of inquiry devoted to living longer bloomed in the twenty-first century—and with it a crop of researchers and scientists, entrepreneurs and athletes, but mostly decamillionaires looking to stand on the forefront of efforts to decelerate age. They want to extend their "health span," stretching their lifespan by decades and their vitality by an order of magnitude.

I met a millionaire recently at a party who said that he wanted to become the longest-living person in history, which I took to be a polite way of saying that he had so much money and time that he didn't know what else to try. But when I read about him later in the newspaper, I discovered that he spent an average day following his custom health protocol, including timing his digestion to maximize his sleep. As a result, his last meal of the day was consumed at a rousing 11:00 A.M.

I asked him if the path to longevity would also lead him to happiness.

"Oh yes," he said. "I am maximizing my potential for happiness, like everything else."

They are their own breed. *Homo immortalitatis cupidus.* Man desirous of immortality.

I used to meet this kind of person all the time when I was interviewing televangelists. I spent my twenties writing a book about the history of the prosperity gospel, and these preachers tended to believe that God promised them so much health, wealth, and happiness that even death would have to wait until they were ready. One of the richest televangelists in the world, Kenneth Copeland, announced as he approached his ninetieth birthday that his soul would not depart his body until 2056, and I had to admit that it was almost fun to watch a man bet against mortality.

This type of person will be the first to tell you that they used to feel the ache. But now they know the formula.

Step one: Improve *everything*.
Step two: Repeat step one.

There are numbers and solutions to almost everything. And for people who love keeping track, happiness represents a kind of *moreness* that comes with more of everything.

Formulas are fixed. They are entirely predictable. You can drag one into a lab in Calgary or Frankfurt or Johannesburg and pick any name from the census and watch how that person, whoever they are, if shown the steps and under the right conditions, will find identical results.

How predictable. How satisfying.

In this telling, there is no mystery.

We simply have to try.

Try, try, try.

There is a wonderful straightforwardness with which we are sold happiness by explaining how to try: try to regulate our eating and sleeping, try to master our emotional responses, try to strive for meaningful work and service, and try to sort out the muss from the fuss from the bother of our relationships. No, it's not easy, they say. But it is a jam sandwich of effort and reward.

Try, try, try.

This is about wanting. This is about you.

14

Is This It?

WE PLUG ALONG and we make our plans. We make more with less—but still, we know:

A small void lies in each of us, and it acts as a perfect echo chamber.

Hope. Fear. Possibility.

There is a longing that rings through us. Is it anxiety? Is it a malaise? Can it simply be solved with some psychological strategies and a little more self-care? Or is this soul work?

As I always do when I can't seem to stop chewing on a question, I turned to research. I went looking for thinkers who had offered their own answers and, after asking around, a name surfaced. *You should talk to Father Ron. He knows all about this. Plus, he's Canadian.* So I reached out to this mysterious Father Ron to see if he might be willing to tell me about his work on longing. It turned out his books have sold a million copies, so he was not so mysterious after all.

Father Ron Rolheiser stared back at me over Zoom from

his office at the Oblate School of Theology, a seminary not unlike my own. He was nearing eighty years old and fending off advanced colon cancer, and I was not about to waste his time. I jumped in immediately.

I asked him about the ache.

"It's the most basic thing about us," he said bluntly. "If you allow me to get philosophical for a minute, remember Descartes's famous line: 'I think, therefore I am.' Saint Augustine argued that's not true. *I desire, therefore I am.* We wake up aching. Just look at the way babies wake up crying and you'll realize that we never really stop for the rest of our lives. There's *always* something missing—that's the deepest truth in my life. And I think it's the deepest truth in everybody's life whether they admit it or not."

Sweet mercy from on high. If I wasn't already sitting, I would have needed to sit down.

I explained how the entire premise felt difficult to admit—that I thought life would feel more meaningful by now, especially given what I had survived. That I had seen too many women weighed down by the cost of being good. That even though I openly despise toxic positivity, I usually lie to people about how terrible I feel. That I keep meeting people who believe that they have cracked the code to happiness and that I am always too tired, too sick, or too overwhelmed to achieve that kind of perfection. And that the things I actually accomplish feel too small to count, especially against the losses that keep stacking up.

That I don't want to ache at all.

"Well," Father Ron said, pausing thoughtfully. "I think a lot of people think it's only a downside. But, in fact, that energy, that perpetual disquiet, that inchoate feeling... it is also divine."

"Wait, say that again?" I asked.

"We are made in the image and likeness of God. So, that feeling isn't a mistake. There's a fire inside of us. But it's a *divine fire*."

"So that feeling I have that I want to swallow the whole world sometimes?" I said, half embarrassed.

"Divine."

"The feeling that I am never, ever at peace?"

"It's a holy longing."

There is that "*Sehnsucht*" feeling—a bittersweet, almost addictive yearning. *Life longings*.

As C. S. Lewis has Psyche say in *Till We Have Faces,* "The sweetest thing in all my life has been the longing."

It is what Henry David Thoreau summarily called our "quiet desperation."

I hear the ache repeat the same question, day after day.

Without an answer.

Is this it? Is this it?Is this it? Is this it? Is this it? Is this it? Is this it? Is this it? Is this it? Is this it? Is this it? Is this it? Is this it? Is this it? Is this it? Is this it? Is this it?

"I guess," I continued slowly, "that makes me irritated by all the false advertising I've been served about being spiritual. I was always taught that faithfulness is the absence of all this longing."

There's a hole in your heart, sure, but that's what God fills. And the more religious you are, the more you know that. Or at least that's what I was promised.

For the last hundred years in particular, there is a particular tone that has overtaken public discourse: absolute certainty. Raw confidence has become the gold standard for moral superiority. You are as good as you are certain. Just take a look at the nicknames of the culture warriors of the last century: The Religious Right. The Moral Majority. These are dramatic statements about righteous people with nothing missing, nothing broken.

I had honestly never imagined that this ache was not a sign of my own weakness. There were moments during cancer when I felt briefly, temporarily whole. But when that feeling left me, I have been lightly haunted by guilt ever since. A better person, a better Christian, a better woman should not need, should not hunger. She would be at peace, right?

"Kate, you and I have suffered too much in our lives to be delusional," he said wryly, which made me laugh. "We need constant encouragement to live with what's never full, what's never complete. Let's remember the insight of the great theologian Karl Rahner: 'In the torment of the insufficiency of everything attainable, we learn that ultimately in this world there is no finished symphony.'"

No finished symphony.

"So, wait, Father Ron," I asked, urgently. "Then what do you do with all the longing?"

"Well, I think that's the very definition of spirituality. It's what we do with that divine fire," he said, and described how some people might use it for unhealthy pursuits of endless more, more, more. Or some people might try to snuff out their own fire in an attempt to be very pious. But that the divine moves through our longing, channeling it toward better and better aims.

"I guess . . . okay, I'll be totally honest: I am much better in a crisis. Spiritually, I mean. I can face down an existential crisis and stare at the apocalypse and feel enormous amounts of love and peace. But then the second that the crisis is over, I feel like such a terrible person. Ordinary life—email, pickups, trying to find a new moisturizer—that stuff makes me feel so itchy. I feel disappointed in myself . . . because I want more. So much more. I feel disappointed about all the places I won't visit. All the careers I will never have. All the things that aren't possible because of *good things,* because of people I love and bills I need to pay. I like your argument that we could channel our spirituality in a certain direction. But can it help me live with not quite so much disappointment or resentment about being SUCH A GOOD PERSON?"

I thought Father Ron would laugh but instead he gave a wonderfully long pause, which is always a great compliment in academic circles. It's like waiting for someone to pull water for you from a deep well.

"We are going to die with a lot of hopes unfulfilled," he said. He might as well have added "*kiddo*" because that's how it felt. *Sorry, kiddo. That's the story.* And that is precisely what a person in their late seventies with advanced cancer and medium-to-low patience should do: tell me the truth.

He continued: "But if you can mourn it, you can live with it. There's a deep spiritual and psychological genius here: I need to mourn this. I can die without being fulfilled, but I can't die with the unfulfillment not being mourned."

I closed my eyes and took a moment to let that thought settle in place. I had been hoping that there was a solution to the ache, but, really, *come on.* When are there hacks—tips and tricks!—to the fundamental questions of our humanity? That's ridiculous. I've never found a shortcut when it comes to genuine, life-altering wisdom. Never, not once.

He was still talking and I wanted to interrupt: "Hey! Quick follow-up, sorry, can I skip right to the joy?"

But I knew the answer already. *Sorry, kiddo. The ache cannot be denied.*

The ache cannot be ignored. Distraction or anger can only get so far . . . so I suppose I would have to be more honest about what I need to grieve. Mourning is the terrible process of allowing reality to wash over you again and again and again.

What do you do when nothing can change but everything must? I will need some help, but at least I know where to start: say yes to the dark unfinishedness of this symphony.

Turn your face toward the ache and say yes.

The ache? *Yes.*

The longing? *Yes.*

The grief? *Yes.*

The holiness of all this want? *I'm not sure how, but yes.*

PART II

Mourning

15

Swifties

THE DURHAM HOTEL rooftop bar was packed. Every patio table was crowded with small plates and surrounded by women—women with blowouts, women in compression jeans, women with their good shoes on. I love the electric energy of women out on the town. It was a night that was going to end in two zillion photos taken (and rejected) for social media or someone using toilet paper to blot mascara tears while protesting, "No, it's good! I'm good."

The sun was slung low, the last remains of its orange glow fading from view behind the red brick factories and tobacco warehouses that once kept this Southern town afloat. The Best Friend and I watched the sun fade at our corner table, mesmerized as swirling black dots moved in synchronous clouds in and out of view. At first glance it looked like swarms of bats infesting the skies of Gotham. But no, it was the great annual migration of the chimney swifts, thousands of tiny birds who take shelter in the downtown chimneys and whose stubby brown bodies have earned them the nickname "The Flying Cigars."

The whole thing was perfectly absurd. The local bird-watching society had struck a deal with the posh downtown hotel, and it had become a bit of a tradition for us to join the crowd to say farewell to the swifts before they migrated to South America. We would raise a glass to the only creature in God's inventory whose sweetest song sounded like tinfoil being rubbed against thousands of cheese graters.

The Best Friend had pulled her hair back in a sleek low ponytail and she gazed out pensively over the city, a salted margarita in her hand and her black turtleneck giving her the air of Steve Jobs on vacation. She was more depressed than I had seen her in a long time.

She had been talking with her especially treasured male friend over FaceTime the other day and it had been implied, not stated, but definitely communicated that he loved her. The conversation had been careful, mannered even, as if clearing a table dish by dish. He was so calm, his voice low and slow, as he placed each of his feelings fully in view. And, looking back, she had been so high off the surrealness of hearing him say anything out loud that the words themselves were soap bubbles that floated away. She couldn't duplicate the conversation for me like we always do—every word, each cadence—except to say he had worn that soft gray T-shirt she loved and he had gotten up to pace a few times because the whole thing was impossible, impossible to imagine, impossible to say. But she was swimming in her own relief. *That's what this is. This is love.*

Then he went silent for a few days, then he texted a joke and a song. Now he was silent again.

I put my hand over her hand, but she hardly noticed. She was staring at her phone as if willing it to light up.

"It must be especially frustrating not to have any opportunity to figure this out with a conversation. He's just . . . gone," I said.

"Exactly. I mean, he could say it was too much or that he wanted to take it back even. I don't know! I genuinely don't know. What am I supposed to do with zero information?" she said hotly, dropping her phone in her purse for emphasis.

"I'm worried this is hurting you so much that it will go on The List," I said, after a time, and she laughed humorlessly.

The Best Friend and I invented The List when we were in college and new to being regularly wronged. The List was a shorthand for the most unfair, most infuriating, most heartbreaking events that life had thrown at us. Something terrible would happen and we would text each other: "Adding this to The List."

Together, we were filing formal paperwork with the Complaints Department of the Universe.

It was never written down, not really, but it was real enough. It was our way of keeping track of the terrible things that happened to us that *really stuck*. Did I have a teenage shouting match with my sister over a Club Monaco shirt? Yes, but that doesn't make the ledger of grievances. Items that make The List are painful, calcified, irrefutable evidence that something bad happened. And it left its mark.

Like the time I paid thousands of dollars to fly out of state to meet with a fancy doctor to ask about my cancer prognosis and he refused to answer, even though it was his specialty and he had a clinical trial running on that very topic. But then he said, philosophically: "What is mortality anyway?"

I told him that it was probably something to do with dying before your kid reaches kindergarten.

Well, that's on The List. That's on The List forever.

It is every major moment that challenged us, changed us, scarred us. And my best friend knows each one, because friends are not simply friends. They are witnesses.

The sounds of salsa music played softly over the loudspeaker and everywhere I looked people were laughing, talking, eating, starring as main characters in their own lives.

"If we were suddenly in a movie, what would we do right now?" I asked abruptly.

"Ummm . . . maybe a buddy cop situation? We are tough-but-fair officers of the law who hunt down complicated friendships, analyzing past conversations and texts and song lyrics in search of secret romantic clues?"

"We are the Ambiguous Friendship Detective Agency," I announced, and we laughed and picked that apart for a bit. Then we walked through our romantic comedy options before settling on the premise that two women go somewhere and unearth a truth about themselves. We will take elaborate and expensive vacations to tropical places where we have confirming experiences about our own gifts, hopes, and attractiveness in an entirely appropriate way. We're not sure how that could happen, but it's some version of *How Stella Got Her Groove Back* for her and *Eat, Pray, Love* for me, but without the love bit.

Drawbacks: Money. Time. Who takes care of the family?

"The other option is self-loathing," I ventured.

"Obviously," she said. We could follow the well-worn path of sudden weight loss and the grave contemplation of adult women getting bangs. Then we would treat tomorrow and the next day and forever like New Year's Day. We would consider the quality of our multivitamins and deep-clean our closets and master every aspect of health and relationships and ambition and domesticity in our domain. We would become disconcertingly charming in the ease with which our perfection is reflected in all our visible and invisible qualities. But mostly visible because we would *definitely* get Botox.

Drawback: Not a robot yet. See also: money, time.

"Or we can give ourselves up altogether, right? Isn't that what every *Little House on the Prairie* character wants? Focus on others. Grow your own . . . I don't know . . . carrots. Care about your family and everything will fall into place," I said, picking up steam. It was an argument whose sweet idealism almost had me convinced: abandon progress and only care about others and their happiness. Disappear into the knowledge that, at its core, life is about love and other people's love is a nuclear power plant. Stop thinking about yourself. Accept the fact that you will never be able to entirely straighten your hair on the parts of your head you can't see. You just can't.

"But I'm absolutely dried up from loving everyone else," she said, putting each word where it belonged. "I'm alone in my apartment. It's fine, truly. But all this, 'You're so brave!' single-lady energy just means that I have to plan my own birthday party and everyone else's, and no one is there to pick me up when I need to leave the car for an oil change."

She was right, of course. I had seen her pick up everyone

else's work assignments and check on people who didn't check on her. This is the question buried at the heart of sacrificial life: when I fall, will someone miraculously be there to lift me up?

I sighed deeply. The ache is deafening for everyone.

"You're right," I said. "That reminds me of the last time I tried to stop thinking about my own needs. I spent most of that summer stopping by the grocery store after work and stress-eating enough chips and guacamole to fill a shipping container until the lifeguard at the local pool asked me not to bring food so close to the water."

Ma'am. Ma'am. That's unsanitary.

"I feel like I'm always trying to make decisions that are best for everyone and none of them are all that great for me," she said, reaching back down into her purse to check her phone again. "It's starting to feel like I'm only really good at mitigating my own losses."

"WELCOME SWIFTIES!" screamed a little black box.

We looked around frantically only to find that a speaker had been placed near our shoes next to the table and, only a foot away, an elderly man was attached to that speaker. The man wore the broad Tilley hat of die-hard bird watchers and a pair of binoculars hung around his neck. He stared blandly back at us.

"SOON YOU WILL LEARN ABOUT THESE INCREDIBLE BIRDS," he said, pressing his mouth against the microphone.

The Best Friend and I exchanged looks. We did want to see these incredible birds take flight, but last year we had done so at our leisure using the power of our eyeballs.

"We're never going to be able to reschedule," she said quickly, which was true. One of the most intimate choices that two friends can make is to share an online calendar. One of us might be saying: "Let's get together!" But our calendars suggest that we expect dental visits, gynecological exams, and math tutoring to be provided at the same facility, ideally by the same practitioner, or else Tuesday is a bust.

"And this is the last table on planet earth," I said. "How long is this going to be?"

"FOR THE NEXT HOUR WE WILL BE CELEBRATING THE ACCOMPLISHMENTS OF THESE ENDANGERED BIRDS."

"Oh, no, no, no." I shook my head.

"What are we going to do?!" she said, looking around to see if others were abandoning their tables. But everyone else was having the time of their lives at a reasonable distance from the speaker system. Dang.

"HERE ARE SOME FACTS! THESE BIRDS ARE HIGHLY GREGARIOUS AND SELDOM ALONE."

The Best Friend and I sat back in our chairs, surrendering to the wall of sound coming out of the man's face. We could barely make out the unusual swift chattering call—high pitched and insistent.

"THEY SHARE CHILD-REARING AMONG THREE TO FOUR ADULTS."

I smiled despite myself. That sounded nice.

"SWIFTS SPEND NEARLY THEIR ENTIRE LIVES IN FLIGHT. EVEN MATING. EVEN EATING. EVEN BATHING."

The ornithologist was pointing now over the railing as the

stubby brown birds swooped in hypnotic circles. There had been heavy rain and the roof of the nearby Mr. Tire Shop had collected thousands of pounds of rainwater into a swimming pool covering the entire length of their building, and, smack, smack, smack, hundreds of birds glided down to take their turn to get clean by whacking their bodies against the surface of the water.

Well, that's relatable, I said to myself, thinking about the five minutes that had been available for me to get ready for tonight with dry shampoo, pants with a button, and lipstick from the center console of my car.

"THEY HAVE ADAPTED TO THE REALITY THAT THEY WILL SPEND MOST OF THEIR LIVES IN FLIGHT. THE MOST REST THEY WILL GET IS A NEST GLUED TO A VERTICAL SURFACE BY SALIVA."

At that the Best Friend and I burst out in peals of laughter. Sometimes you will be stuck flying endless long distances. Sometimes your day will be determined by horrifying efficiency. Sometimes your "best life now" might be the moment you look around and see a group of swifties flying with you.

But surely there has got to be some way to stop feeling like every day is a round-robin of obligations. I know how to love the people I've been given—I can do that—but can I imagine a life that is more than simply Exhaustion Management? I looked at my little Steve Jobs beside me and had a thought, which I had to shout to be heard above the noise. She leaned in to hear me.

"I WANT MORE THAN A LIFE GLUED TOGETHER BY SALIVA!" I yelled.

"Ha! Ha! YES!" she yelled back.

"I WANT SOMETHING GOOD TO HAPPEN! I WANT JOY!" I shouted.

The bird expert was glaring at us now owing to what had become a fairly even competition for the airwaves.

"FATHER RON TOLD ME TO START GRIEVING!"

The moment I said it I realized I didn't even know where to start. This feeling had been such a constant presence that it almost felt like a part of my personality. *What do I even want? What am I allowed to want?*

I don't know. I honestly don't know. But if Father Ron was right, then the first place to look would be the worst things that ever happened.

The List!

"MAYBE WE SHOULD START WITH GRIEVING THE LIST!" I yelled, thoughtfully, all things considered.

She nodded and a look of recognition flashed across her face. "THEN MAYBE WE SHOULD FINALLY WRITE IT DOWN!"

I nodded a bit too enthusiastically given the apocalyptic tenor. Yes. We could start with the memories that still made our blood boil. It had become such a wonderful shorthand for our righteous anger: "This happened. It was huge. It was unfair." There was comfort in that too. And even a protective shield against further pain.

The problem, however, was that there were that many problems in the first place. The number of difficult experiences that we had endured was getting larger and larger; they were accumulating on us like barnacles on a hull. It was as if Tennyson had indicted us when he wrote, "I am a part of all that I have met." The Complaints Department logbook was growing and I was afraid that it was starting to make us into the kind of people who repeat the same stories, the same complaints, not because we love them, but because pain had become a familiar friend.

What would grieving The List do exactly? Perhaps it won't erase what happened or even lessen the burden, but could it make room for something more?

Even as I considered it, I could feel myself rejecting the thought.

Sorry, Serenity Prayer. I do not want to accept the things I cannot change. I want to rage against them.

I looked over at my friend staring back at me, her eyes constantly pulled toward the home screen of her phone. He loved her. Or, at least, he loved her *almost* enough to stop the pain. I had the distinct impression that in a week he would text again and send her another song and she would stay glued to him with saliva forever.

The sun had almost entirely disappeared behind the buildings now, and the crimson red of the hundreds of chimneys in this Southern town faded to gray. If I squinted, I could make out the blackened silhouettes of thousands of moving flecks still dancing above them.

Perhaps there is some wisdom in motion. When we find ourselves swept up in a current that we can't control, perhaps all that's left to do is stretch out our wings. Find the wind. Feel yourself adjusting course. But let yourself only be swept along as far as you must, and not an inch more, because it's time to fight like hell.

It won't always be this way, but today it is. Two friends anchored together on the rooftop while the last light slips away and the swifts find their nests. One of us will cry again before we leave ("I'm fine! I'm fine!") and the other will insist that we get another round. I will threaten to throw her phone off the balcony, but I will relent to reviewing the lyrics of the last song he sent ("He loves me, right? Like I'm not making that up?"). And we will raise our glasses to the conclusions we settled on tonight, which will come up again with the sun tomorrow:

Here's to the endurance of every kind of swiftie!
Here's to the pain! Here's to the joy!
But first, here's to the grief.

16

The List: Recent Filings to the Complaints Department

General rules for making a list of your own grievances: (1) Start with stories you repeat. If it wasn't important, you probably wouldn't be telling it for the zillionth time to the person next to you on a plane. (2) Be specific. (3) Be more honest than you want to be. (4) Name names! Someone didn't hurt you in general. It was Linda! (5) Don't worry about feeling like a good person. You're not trying to win Miss Congeniality. Only Sandra Bullock can be Sandra Bullock.

1. Wishing I had grown up with a Restaurant Family. Restaurant Family (def): any family, anywhere, that doesn't need to sequester someone in the car before the check comes because of an argument.

2. All the doctors who didn't believe me and who sent me home with Pepto Bismol when I had Stage IV cancer. And especially the doctor with meatball eyes who was fine letting me die philosophically.

3. The frustrating silence around my last set of scans and how I let Peter, Paul, and Mary pretend that I am capable of handling it alone. No one is. Why am I managing other people in the middle of my own crisis?

4. Overcaring about the pettiest parts of my job when I promised myself when I was sick that I would never do that again.

5. The general fact that most women are better at being married than being happy.

17

Anybody?

I WROTE THE LIST in black ink in the leatherbound diary I normally keep beside my bed. It took the better part of an hour and a lot of staring into the distance followed by some quick calls to The Best Friend to see if I had left anything off.

I probably had.

There is something really strange that happens when you actually write out the list, when you find yourself looking at a catalog of heartbreaks.

"Let no one lightly set about such a work," says Queen Orual when she sets down to write her own list in the novel *Till We Have Faces*. "Memory, once waked, will play the tyrant."

The first thing you notice is that the words seem strange. Did that really happen?! You were there, you know it did. But it has become harder and harder to feel the seriousness of it. When you see the words written down, gravity shifts. The words take on weight. Pain is formed in discrete moments, and that sinking feeling in your chest? Grief. Because you actually believe what you have written. *Now you know all over again.*

Let's say you have sat with these moments for years. You have even reexamined a few of them until, on closer reflection, there were some hidden revelations. You learned patience. You learned fortitude. You learned how to carry heavy boxes of everything you've ever loved out of a place you never wanted to leave without tweaking your back. Well, well, well. That really is incredible. You congratulate yourself for having plucked diamonds from the furnace, clawed insight from the wreckage of disaster after disaster. You tell your psychologist named Henry who has heard about these difficult memories every time you visit his office full of tapestries from Arizona. Has he mentioned he is from Arizona? He has.

But then you take that precious list into the living room and start to read it (carefully, instructively, sometimes loudly) to your husband, parents, and friends. You find yourself bringing it up again the next day, in the course of what was supposed to be a casual conversation about your birthday. ("Remember when last year was quantifiably worse because of *that thing you did*?") Soon you discover that the next great revelation is about to take place: no one cares.

"Aren't you over that by now? And, I mean, haven't we sort of heard that story before? It sounds familiar. And didn't we sort of apologize? *Sort of.* And don't you feel better?"

NO I DO NOT.

Right at the time you have realized that this little list contains burdens that have altered the course of your human life, you feel the shrug of it all. You feel the bland commiseration of others.

Also, sorry, what about blame? Researcher Brené Brown (blessed be her name) made me think differently about shame, but who will deputize me to lead a cultural movement of blame? Rise up, wronged of the earth! I don't want to put a percentage on it, but, if pressed, didn't 99 percent of suffering come from someone else's inexcusable behavior?

There's a simple solution to my problems: everyone else. Everyone else could improve significantly. Period. End of problems.

After the mania of wishing you could wake up to an entirely different and apologetic world, a fresh wave of sadness comes. Or, worse, you suddenly despise your own weakness. You might look at your own list—your own deepest sadness—and hate it. Hate the list, hate everyone, hate yourself. Isn't it so terribly embarrassing? The way stories from the past have taken on a future of their own? And isn't *whining* the least attractive verb in the English language? At least the British call it "whinging" for the depressing effect of listening to someone belabor a grievance.

Sometimes I find myself in the middle of a story about how the wild and pernicious neglect of the healthcare system, you know, led to my Stage IV cancer diagnosis—and I'm bored. I'm actually boring myself mid-speech. Ultimately pain is the strangest combination of dull and urgent and mortifying and something I cannot wait to volunteer before you ask me.

And then he said . . .

And then I said . . .

George Orwell once observed that pain only makes you want one thing: "that it should stop. Nothing in the world was so bad as physical pain. In the face of pain there are no heroes."

Why then do we wish we were heroic?

In these terrible moments you could almost hope that a hospital staff member would pop up with her ubiquitous pain scale.

"On a scale of one to ten, how much does this hurt?"

AT LEAST A SEVEN, JENNIFER.

In the face of suffering, we are laid low. We are humbled. We are humiliated by having lost control of our own futures. And we look around in hopes that someone else has seen it too.

I think *that* is the part of growing and changing that makes me feel like I want to crawl out of my own skin: there will be no witness.

When we really look at the list, when we see clearly the pain that has made us who we are, we see also that we are alone.

There is only you.

Only you, standing there with a slightly deranged expression, saying, *does anyone else see this? Feel that?*

Anybody?

18

This Is Not Codependency

"It's the most natural thing in the world, the desire to be happy."

A fresh-faced employee is explaining the premise of one of the retreats—The Art of Happiness—being offered at the wellness resort where I'll be staying for a couple days on a research trip. These new arrivals shouldn't forget to sign up for activities like yoga and meditation, she insists. You can even make pottery here on the grounds. The group was buzzing, sifting through their welcome material and peeling away momentarily to ask questions. *Are our rooms far from here? Would it be possible to do a sunrise hike?* As the noise continued to rise, the employee reached out her hands pressed together with a prayerful combination of peace-be-with-you and shush-your-face.

"All your questions are going to be answered. But the real answer is: yes! Yes, you're going to find peace here. Yes, you're going to find direction here. And happiness . . ." She smiled again. "It's practically automatic."

I couldn't help but look over from the check-in desk when I heard her, and she was every bit as radiant as she sounded. How old was she? I guessed from her ponytail and the post-college intern labor pool that these retreat centers usually employ that she could not have been more than twenty-five. I sighed. If it is one thing I miss from being young, it's not the shared family cell phone plan: it's the certainty.

The retreat center was a charming and bustling place that hosts thousands of guests each month on its sprawling campus wedged into a soft peak of one of the Blue Ridge Mountains, the sloping range that climbs up the eastern states and whose crowded horizon of trees glows an eerie turquoise. And this weekend was one of many that I was going to spend studying spiritual views about happiness for a forthcoming historical book I was writing. In an average year, I spend a few hundred hours listening to people explain how their faith can solve the problem of suffering, and I, in turn, try to represent their views fairly in the scholarly books I write for university audiences.

Much of my historical research on modern religious communities tends to focus on the development of cultural myths about health, wealth, and the American Dream, but mostly I find myself wondering if people can get out of their own way enough to be happy at all.

Maybe people don't change. Right? Or maybe no one lets us change. And we stay the same because we are with the same people forever.

Normally a weekend of academic work requires that I do a lot of interviewing, but this retreat center offered the option of taking a vow of delicious silence and, after having unsuccessfully tried to review my List of Complaints with my husband, parents, and co-workers, I could not have been more grateful for some fresh mountain air and the promise of a 9:00 P.M. bedtime. There is nothing I have come to cherish more than respite disguised as a work trip.

I took my book of poetry and sat down in the airy cafeteria next to a placard that read QUIET PLEASE.

Almost immediately a husband and wife plopped down beside me, leaving the rest of the long rectangular table empty and undisturbed.

The man, thin as a pipe cleaner, bent himself over his tray and set to work pushing plump pieces of tofu around his cardboard bowl with a spoon. He sighed.

"He doesn't like tofu," his wife said, ignoring the QUIET sign with the urgency of a spouse unwilling to live alone with this information for a moment longer.

They were a classic pairing: an engine and a brake. She was only a day into the conference but was already sporting one of the center's branded lotus flower T-shirts from The Heavenly Gift Shop and her graying curls were slick with sesame oil from a therapeutic oil drip at the Ayurvedic Wellness Center. He, on the other hand, glowered with the resentment of the freshly conscripted.

I set down my book reluctantly.

"Are you having a good time?" I asked.

"He doesn't like tofu," she said again, this time a little louder, as she struggled to be heard above the rising noise. A large group of women poured through the doors and lined up at the enormous vegetarian buffet. She turned to her husband. "Why don't you go ask the kitchen for something different? They are here to make sure you are happy with what you're eating. They *want* to help you." She glanced at me. "I'm not doing this."

"What brought you here?" I asked the husband, a little hopeful for a change in topic.

The man shrugged.

"Happiness?" he answered, doubtfully. "Happiness is important."

I glanced around and began to number the gray heads. This was the Beatles generation, the first to mainstream meditation and yoga and spiritual bliss with an Eastern twist. Baby boomers had been promised all the freedom of nonconformity and every winding therapeutic and spiritual and psychedelic path to achieve individual happiness. And now with the great transition to retirement, I wondered if the 1970s had lived up to the spiritual promises it made them in their extended adolescence.

"What do you think of the yoga here? Any good?"

He shrugged again, but it looked like a yes.

"There should be a sound bath tomorrow. I heard those are very interesting."

"Yes."

"I'd like to try the pottery classes."

He stopped fishing in his soup enough to give me a long look, and I decided, definitively, that I am an irritating person. But then he answered.

"Everything is perspective. You have to tell a story about

reality. And this is reality, and I need to tell *this* story. I'm seventy-one. I'm retired, but . . . not really. I'm relaxing. Can't you tell?" He raked his hand through his sparse hair, which stuck up like alfalfa, but he had now shifted his disappointed attention back to his paper dish. His shoulders slumped again.

"I'M NOT DOING THIS," his wife chimed in, louder.

He looked up evenly and they stared at each other across the table. Then she looked at me.

"I'm learning *a lot* about acts of loving-kindness. My husband is older than me and he's retired. Did you hear that, honey? You are *retired*. This is *slowing down*."

She returned her focus to me. "We are figuring out how this is going to work. This is . . . our new way of being together." She said the last bit slowly, as if she was beginning to believe what she was saying for the first time. "BUT I AM NOT CODEPENDENT. THIS IS NOT CODEPENDENCY. DO YOU WANT ME TO ASK THE KITCHEN FOR BEANS?"

The man looked up suddenly and smiled for the first time in our interminable lunch together. "Yes, please," he said sweetly. And she stomped off to the kitchen and, far in the distance, I could hear a door slam. He put his fork down when he heard it. We both paused.

"Happiness is really important," he said abruptly, returning to our conversation as if ending a philosophical debate between us. He nodded toward where his wife had disappeared into the kitchen. "Because no one likes a grouchy person. No one."

19

Highly Sensitive People

"Did everyone take the diagnostic test?"

Hands went up. The email explaining the criteria for admission into the Highly Sensitive Leader Book Club had been aggressively bolded and underlined with threats about being underprepared followed by encouragement to "reply all" with responses to questions like *Do other people's moods affect you deeply? Are you made uncomfortable by loud sounds? Do you worry that you said the wrong thing long after a social situation is over?*

It was a surprisingly intimate set of prompts given the circumstances. But I was feeling indicted by the recent revelation that I would probably *also* volunteer to solve a man's need for beans instead of tofu, so, yes: *Other people's moods do affect me deeply.*

I had heard about this group a month ago, when I attended a leadership conference that included military generals and senators and CEOs, and none of it had been particularly personal. I had worn a lot of pantsuits and tried to promote a general sense of my authority by starting sentences with "Research shows that . . ." and, my personal favorite, "It was the nineteenth century and . . ." But a follow-up email had encouraged us to join a series of book clubs, and I had been particularly interested in the one that was reading the psychologist Elaine Aron's bestselling book *The Highly Sensitive Person*. The book claimed that a whopping 20 percent of people are highly sensitive and need to learn to live with the many gifts and burdens that come along with it. Frankly, I saw a lot of burdens and not a lot of gifts, so I was intrigued.

A woman in her twenties adjusted her camera, her eyes darting around the screen. There were five of us on Zoom sitting in our air-conditioned offices scattered around the country, and I didn't recognize anyone from the conference. "I think we're all here. Okay? Welcome. This is an invitation-only group and the purpose today is to explore our highly sensitive qualities in relationship to our leadership styles. We'll only be meeting this one time, so we ask for one hundred percent participation, okay? I'm your moderator."

I shifted in my office chair uncomfortably. What is worse than an average day of feeling the pain of everyone around me? Maybe sitting in a group therapy meeting with other people making each other equally miserable. It was like we all decided to hold hands and benevolently electrocute ourselves.

"Let's start with the results then. How many people scored ten or higher?"

Everyone's hands went up again.

"Why don't we introduce ourselves and say which diagnostic question seemed *especially* true to you? Kate, why don't you start us off?" she prodded.

Now that we were saying words like *diagnostic test* I started to feel the need to have quibbles about the research protocol. But fine.

"I'm Kate," I began. "I think of myself as someone who has too much 'When is the pizza coming?' energy. Just useless amounts of alertness to the needs around me. If someone has a problem, I find it almost impossible to calm down and be happy."

Everyone nodded.

I immediately wanted to tell them a follow-up about the time my mother (who really *is* a highly sensitive person) had last been made uncomfortable by loud sounds—even though she is a professional singer. She had asked someone to turn the music down. And that someone did not feel the need to ask for a manager or even glance around to meet someone else's eye in a gesture of silent commiseration. There was only the faintest trace of a piano over the loudspeaker and an ancient customer in a jewel-toned blazer scraping her walker over the floor.

"Ma'am," said the woman, looking my mother dead in the eye. "This is *Talbots*."

But I kept my mouth shut.

"I'm Ruth." The woman was perhaps in her early sixties and had the disappointed expression of someone never in control of the office thermostat. "I am the chief science officer for an organization you've probably heard of . . ." She trailed off knowingly.

Everyone else laughed. My hands reached for the keyboard

to start an internet search, but we were firmly instructed to keep the microphone off mute.

"I had an idyllic childhood in many ways," Ruth continued. "Wonderfully attentive parents. Who else had parents who would quiz them on words like 'orogeny'?"

This time I knew when to laugh.

"But then I began school. And realized that I was . . . a genius."

I laughed loudly, but the faces were somber, concerned.

"It didn't help that I could read everyone else's emotions so easily. Especially my sister's. She was jealous, I mean, how could she not be? But she was the one with all the friends. I felt . . . this whole thing . . . it's been very lonely." Her voice began to tremble. "I'm sorry," she whispered.

The moderator nodded for a good long while. "Thank you, Ruth.

"How many other people connect to Ruth's feeling that she can read everyone else's emotions in the room? Yes? Everyone? It's a common trait for highly sensitive people, or HSPs as they are sometimes called."

I mean, I thought I had *already* said that, but that's fine. We can all be happy for Ruth and her experiences.

There were nods all around.

"My name is Ava," said a woman. She was very pale and freckled, her thin hair pulled back into a ponytail, her small frame hunched making her appear even smaller. "I'm on my *third* start-up."

There were a lot of murmurs of approval for that. The only man on the Zoom looked at her with particular pride. It is commonly said that one successful start-up makes you lucky, two makes you a legend, but three makes you a genius. I shook my head. I guess I had stumbled into a real tar pit of genius here.

"I've been able to use my intuition to make quick pivots in my business. But I'm . . . it's too much." She cupped her head in her hands and rubbed her temples. "I've had weeks in intensive therapy situations and retreat centers. I know *why* I have this gift. I had an alcoholic mother, and I'm gifted at anticipation. But it's been a tremendous source of pain in my life too."

I felt like I could feel her humming through the screen, that poor little sparrow.

"Has anyone else done the Enneagram test?" I asked. Everyone shook their heads.

"What's the premise?" asked Ruth.

"There are nine types of people and each of them has a primary motivation. So I'm an Enneagram 2, which means I am the helper type. Compassionate. People-pleasing. And I will die of empathy-related causes."

Ava was the only one who laughed, but who would keep track of something like that?

"Did you want to say anything, Todd?" inserted the moderator.

"Yeah, sure." Todd had an enormous Mitt Romney face. He was handsome and at ease, and whenever he spoke, it sounded like he was leaning back. "My name is Todd and I'm a venture capitalist."

We waited for more, but Todd looked down and seemed to hammer something out on his phone just out of view.

Ava shook her head, imperceptibly annoyed, and then leaned toward the camera. "I read a quote the other day that said, 'You're safe. You can let go.' I would really like to do that but I'm struggling with *how*."

"Awareness of other people's nonverbal cues has made leadership very difficult for me," Ruth affirmed. "I find that after a big meeting I am absolutely emotionally exhausted."

"I had a really big meeting," Todd piped in. "I was interviewing someone for a new position and right before he pulled up in his Uber, there was another car that rammed right into the stop sign in front of my building. BAM!" He clapped his hands together and we all startled.

"Oh no!" exclaimed Ava, looking even more pale than before. "Are you okay? That must have been terrifying."

"I guess the driver had a stroke or something but he was going so fast he flipped the car. Man! It was crazy!" said Todd, shaking his head and grinning.

"Has anyone else connected their sensitivity to difficult life experiences?" said the moderator, nudging the conversation back on track. "Emotional chaos or feeling too much can start early in childhood."

"Well, I did read an interesting book the other day called *The Drama of the Gifted Child* by Alice Miller," said Ruth. "And it was talking about how highly sensitive and perceptive kids often adapt to meet their parents' emotional needs. But it comes at a steep cost to themselves."

"But the benefit is that we are better than other people, right?" I joked.

"Right," Ava laughed.

"When the guy I was interviewing got there, I was actually in the upside-down car cutting the driver out of his seatbelt with my pocketknife," said Todd at a nice healthy volume.

Ava sighed.

I paused and considered them both again. Ava must have known Todd a long time, because she rolled her eyes. "Of course you had a pocketknife," she said.

"But the ambulance came?!" asked Ruth, whose turn it was to be deeply alarmed. She was visibly drained by each new detail.

"I was doing chest compressions by then. It's fine," he said blandly. "I was in the marines."

We took in that information with remarkable nonchalance.

There was a pause then, as perhaps we were all sensing that the moderator should make a return to the argument. But the moderator only said, "What happened to the guy you wanted to interview?"

"Oh!" said Todd, delighted. "I did the whole interview. Up in my office. I mean, I started doing the interview, but the guy looked so spooked and then I looked down and realized, oh man, I am covered in blood. So I asked someone for an extra shirt and finished it up and BAM!" He slapped the table again, and we still jumped. "Can you believe it? What a day!"

"Wait," said Ava, sitting up at full height. "This was *today*?! And what happened to the guy?"

"I hired him!"

"THE GUY IN THE CAR, TODD!" fumed Ava.

"Oh! I don't know. I think his heart had probably stopped

by the time he got to the hospital." Todd shrugged. "I've had people die in my arms before, and, honestly, it's a gift. I feel *nothing*."

Ava looked homicidal. Anemic, but homicidal. I pushed in. "Todd, would you say that you are a pretty sensitive person?"

"Oh yeah," he said. "That's what this is about."

"It is," said the moderator, at last. "And how can we help you most right now?"

"Todd," Ava interrupted, coming in hot. "You are completely detached. I've never seen you in possession of a single emotion that I would even recognize as compassion. You can't even put photos of your parents up in your house. You can't say 'I love you.' Dude."

Even the moderator dropped any pretense of not being incredibly interested in this turn of events. When had they broken up?

"No, I'm sensitive!" protested Todd. "I'm here! I'm here because . . . I'm giving out awards to some of my employees, and I noticed that I have a hard time complimenting people." There was a flicker of uncertainty in his eyes as he registered that this might not have been the emotional reveal we had expected.

Ava put her head in her hands, while Ruth, Moderator Girl, and I could not keep our eyes off of Todd's beautiful and dumbfounded face.

A terrible silence ensued and held.

"Ruth," I said, suddenly remembering, "what was the cost to the gifted child?"

"Oh," she said, reluctantly breaking the tension in the atmosphere. "I think it was that the child learns a 'poisonous pedagogy' of psychologically harmful repression of her own needs and grows up presenting a false self to the world."

"Ah," I said. "So who is worse? The person who has no feelings at all and pretends they care? Or the person who secretly resents everyone she cares about?"

I was talking about myself, but Ava looked up at that moment and burst into deep laughter that devolved into coughing. Todd smiled sheepishly, still not sure if or what would take him off the hook.

"Oh," said Ava, wiping her eyes. "I think we're all the worst."

20

Poisonous Pedagogy

We are not simply born. We become.

This is existentialist philosopher Simone de Beauvoir's famous insight about how a woman is made, bit by bit, layer by layer, through small gestures, middling expectations, and constant calibration. We learn. We learn to flatter and please and listen. We learn to get out of the way of other people's disapproval. We fold ourselves up into the most delicate origami, every tight corner. We are taught to worship at the altar of the greatest cause of all: emotional equilibrium.

It will be years before we learn the truth: the world teaches us to read the room before we read ourselves.

Is this how a sensitive child becomes an embittered adult?

I learned early that my feelings were too loud. The lessons came quietly but persistently: don't cry so much, don't care so much, don't want so much. I believed that I had been afflicted by a disease called Too Muchness. I have seen the same affliction in people who were forced to act as caregivers—parenting their parents—before they were in any position to take on that responsibility. When Ruth described her own fears about her sensitivity, I went to read the book she had recommended. Psychologist Alice Miller described what happens to children who learn this poisonous pedagogy: they internalize the message that their exuberance and pain are both excessive and unwelcome.

I know that during difficult times I have believed those words: *I am the bad thing. I am a problem to be solved.* This is why we store away our honest resentments in the first place. Who even wants to hear this?

My emotional vigilance did not dissipate with adulthood; it simply changed form. I become someone else's weather vane. Feminist theorists call this "emotional labor" or, more precisely, "hermeneutic labor": the exhausting work of interpreting and managing not only my own feelings but my partner's. Though I'm not sure what I would call the annoyance with which I once stood over my husband's sleeping body waiting for him to wake up so I could make the bed.

There is a terrible mystery at the heart of an overfunctioning life: what happens if I stop?

I know the answer: everything—everyone—would have to change. The promises of feminism would be magically fulfilled. A generation of men raised on video games would end the longest adolescence in human history. I should have listened to my friend Kristen Howerton, a marriage and family therapist, when she warned that Gen X marriages are a steaming pile of unrealized promises of egalitarian partnership because *they have never seen it modeled.*

Who else would need to change?

Me. Definitely me.

A marital therapist asked me once how I felt when my husband was unhappy and without thinking I cried: "It's unbearable!" Oh boy. But it did explain why I have spent entire weekends irritating myself by attempting to manage my feelings *through* his feelings—my needs *through* his needs—and then I become certain that I am my mother. I was keeping the house quiet in my own way.

There is a cost to feeling too much. But there is also a cost to feeling too little.

I asked some female friends if we could keep ourselves in check with some easy diagnostic questions:

- Did you call him a hero for displaying normal emotional range?

- Did you make all the vacation plans and then congratulate him when he was VAGUELY AWARE of what was happening?

- Did you let him guilt you into believing that an evening without pickleball is a human rights violation?

- When he had garbage in his hands, did you reach out to collect it from him?

We instituted the Garbage Test after I discovered that I was voluntarily opening the chip bags of anyone on an airplane who looked like my dad. *Humiliation, thy name is Doritos.* I need to exit this superhighway, paved in childhood, that drives straight past my own worries to someone else's comfort. I need to find different strategies to unplug from other people's feelings. Because, as it stands, the only surefire way I know to avoid paying granular attention to my husband's moods and disappointments is to leave the house for work.

I will stop aching when everyone else stops.

Sometimes it feels like that is my one true religion: I will shield you from pain. And as a parent, it feels like a sacred vow. "You're only as happy as your unhappiest child," the saying goes, and it is both a warning and a curse. The tragedy—if that's not too grand a word—emerges most sharply in motherhood. I want my child to be emotionally agile, feel everything, express himself fully. But the moment I see his discomfort: "unbearable" again. I hover, I fix, I absorb. I have become an anxious embodiment of the words *Let me help you . . .*

Many wiser than me have tried this before.

The famed novelist and theologian Frederick Buechner was watching his teenage daughter suffer with anorexia. She was being whittled down to bones and a feeding tube, and, in his helplessness, all he could do was suffer with her. To feel her pain. To watch her living death. To be consumed by the hours of fitful worry and arguments with healthcare providers and emergency trips to the hospital. And he began to lay down a rule for himself: "I had no right to be happy unless the people I loved—especially my children—were happy too."

But the work of bubble-wrapping every human heart in love and protection . . . it never ends. It never, ever, ever ends. Further, this desire to give and give can bring its own perversity. I could hear it when I was talking with a friend, Amanda Doyle, who is a lawyer and passionate activist for other people's deepest good. We were discussing how stressful it feels to stop obsessively patrolling other people's needs. Then she asked the perfect questions: When did I decide everyone *else* gets my best gifts? Why is my light always facing out and never in?

Perhaps this is why I recently bought an embroidered pillow that reads I AM NOT NEEDY. I AM WANTY.

There must be a gentler path to love, love of others, love of ourselves. All I know is whenever I have tried, it has felt strange and selfish and wrong to get back what I have given. And it would require more honesty about my disappointments than I have yet been willing to tolerate.

But wouldn't it be so sad, in the end, to have missed out on our own high esteem? To have left to rot so much of our own good and lovely gifts because we were too frantic to give each one of them away?

21

The Leaky Heart

THE BEST FRIEND and her magically platonic friend had been talking again and then, one night, they talked for so long they fell asleep on the phone and when she woke up, he was still there, snoring softly. It was heaven.

She was careful, so careful, about the way she talked to him, but then one day she wasn't careful at all. "I wish you would come see me," she said. "I know you're busy, but I don't want to be the one making all of the effort." Then came the silence. Then came the pleading—was she pleading? She couldn't tell. He seemed to have formed an opinion he never told her. She pressed him for a conversation and when he finally called, he repeated the only unkind thing he had ever said to her: that she was not special.

"I'm not a special person," she told me later that night. "He said he has a lot of important people in his life, and it's like the alphabet. That he will get to me when he runs through the letters and gets to my name." It was such a specific and stupid thing to say that I almost laughed, but she looked like she was still turning it over and over.

I wanted to say that he sounded like a selfish prick, frankly.

"But you haven't done anything wrong," I reasoned. "Maybe he can decide that it's a bit much, or scale it back, or ramp it up, but why would he say something that's so obviously a lie?"

"I don't know," she said. "I don't know. But I am wrong somehow."

She said the word *wrong* like she had struck a bell.

"How can *you* be wrong, my love?"

She started to say it at the close of every long conversation on the phone, when we were in the final adjudication of the weights and measures of a day. At a distance now, she was watching the world in love. How tables have two chairs. How every book she pulled off the shelf was about hearts tested but never conquered. She had come to believe that if she were perfect—if she were not *wrong* somehow—that she would not ache. It is a kind of fiction of completeness sold to us at every turn.

Of course we have the longing to be known and loved and cherished. I remember a conversation I had with an actress who wanted to fall in love, and I asked her what she would look for. She said, "I want him to say, 'I love your pointy teeth. Your weird and pointy teeth.'" And she curled her fingers up in front of her face like badger fangs.

We need someone to love all our badger fangs. And then, for a moment, it's true that the sheer existence of that person walking the earth will fill us with delight.

"What was it?" I asked the Best Friend one night. "What

did he do that was so special?" I am trying to tell her that she is still whole, even if he is the last person to make her feel that way. I want to tell her that he is not the secret to the universe, *she is*.

"He let me finish every sentence," she said, quietly. Long ago, the first time they stayed up late at night talking, he let her finish every sentence, and then tell him the one after *that*. She settled on that memory with a kind of wonder. Her mind was luxuriously empty, having poured it all out. The feeling of having stepped beyond the entirety of her imagination with an outstretched hope that she was not alone, never alone, in whatever occurred to her next.

There is a quality of silence that can shut the valves of a leaky heart. But tonight as we walked and talked and walked and talked, the crickets nattered on and the fascism of suburban nocturnal watering restrictions kept the sprinklers tick, tick, ticking, and stray trucks whooshed down the arterial highway in the distance, there would be no conspiracy to give her back her peace.

22

Below Sea Level

YEARS AGO I visited the northern reaches of the Netherlands, far away from the famous canal houses of Amsterdam, all the way north to the Wadden Sea. My husband and I were visiting his family there, and his uncle Bert—a vision in John Lennon glasses and a full imperial beard—toured us around the coastline in his micro-car. *Meep meep.*

Intellectually I knew that the Netherlands' name means "low-lying country." But Uncle Bert liked to lecture as he drove, and it had been very interesting to learn that since the late sixteenth century, and, really, since the beginning of Dutch history, citizens had been building and maintaining elaborate drainage systems, dikes, canals, and embankments that had made what was essentially an alluvial flood plain into an engineering marvel. Huge swaths of the population now live on land reclaimed from the ocean.

But barely.

We parked the car and with the wind too loud for us to

really talk, we stood silently facing the choppy waters of the Wadden Sea. "Look there," said Uncle Bert with an enormous gesture, pointing to where a hundred-year-old seawall stretched out a thin arm. I had read somewhere that climate change and rising seas levels were prompting a flurry of new talks for a multi-million-dollar renovation. Uncle Bert took a few steps further, and I watched him consider the infrastructure with pride and concern.

For as long as I can remember, the floods have always come.

I grew up on the prairie plains of Manitoba where the waters rise steeply, suddenly, and the cities and towns must attempt anything to stop them. The white snow would melt into the muddy brown of the Red River, which would creep over its boundaries and up to the edges of the highways, and the schools would empty to give us over to sandbagging. School buses would have to be driven south of the city and toppled over, and bulldozers would heap as much dirt on top of them as possible to build a wall. And when everything had been done and all the groceries were stocked up in a fridge that might yet lose power, we would watch and wait and watch and wait.

I always wish I could explain this feeling to strangers, to friends. I would tell them, like the artist Sara Groves sings: "Some hearts are built on a floodplain."

There are moments in our lives when we must admit that almost nothing can change. Not everything is possible. A few variables will remain in our control but the rest is luck or chance or the snow melt or God.

That is the heart of almost every question I bring to my

research about health and wealth and guaranteeing *anything*. How do we discern what is in our control and what is not?

But here is what cancer and suffering and aging and resentment and The List and everything big and small has taught me: complete control is an illusion. It is a beautiful lie. Grief will teach us this lesson again and again.

When we cannot do anything else with our ache, we might rage and cry and make plans and get a tattoo. But if we start to repeat again that "Anything is possible!" then grief has not been invited to stay.

We only begin to grieve when we believe—when we know in our bones—that it doesn't matter what we do. We can like it or not. We can face it or not. We can make our peace with it or allow it to haunt us to the end. But reality persists.

I believe that life can be full of stunning beauty and maybe even a miracle or two, but for the most part it will be lived on a floodplain.

"It is easy to forget that we are below sea level," Uncle Bert explained when we got back into the car, the wind still ringing in our ears. "But this life, ours, will require constant maintenance."

And I glanced back at the receding view of the ocean, vast and greedy.

23

Pruning Shears

THE NEW HOUSE stood at the end of a crescent-shaped street, its brick exterior unassuming among a patchwork of similar homes. The neighborhood seemed quiet, punctuated by the occasional dog walker or passing car, but since our family was pulling up the driveway for the eighth time that day, the novelty was most certainly wearing off.

I had once dreamed of seeing movers trailing in and out of the house like ants, but no. My husband, Toban, was going through another one of his Canadian fits of belief that everything has to be done for free, so we were moving ourselves, box by box, across town. I hopped out of the passenger side of his truck and folded down the tailgate and stared at the pile, which seemed to have grown in the hour since our last trip. I suppressed a sigh. After fifteen years, we had accumulated a lot of *stuff*, but since I had been out of town for the last couple days, I was not in any position to lecture him on the fact that there were twelve more truckfuls left to schlep.

I pulled out my phone to look for immediate validation.

> **Me**
> I can't believe we are living only three minutes apart now.

> **Best Friend**
> Don't be too happy. My neighbor sprays deer urine on his balcony plants every night.

> **Me**
> WHAT? WHY?

> **Best Friend**
> Well it can't be for safety, because I'm going to kill him.

I pulled a few cardboard boxes toward me, handed one to Zach (who immediately began using it as a battering ram), another couple to Toban, and we juggled them through the doors. Inside, the rooms were naked except for the piles and piles of more brown cardboard. I emptied my arms onto the kitchen counter—spare, practical, and currently home to a half-eaten granola bar—and turned around to give everyone instructions, but Zach was off like a shot.

"I'll call this the *hallway of doom*!" yelled Zach from somewhere upstairs, rattling the iron bars of a balcony and, I hoped, finding it structurally sound.

I nudged the open box nearest to me with my foot. A frying pan. Several unmatched shoes. Dishwashing detergent.

My flat iron. And, yes, inexplicably, there they were. My acne patches. I eyed my husband for a long moment.

"Toban, when I was gone, did you have help packing these boxes?"

Toban pressed his lips together in a bland smile, the way he does when he knows that withholding information will be incredibly irritating to me.

"I'm just really noticing a theme to this box," I pressed.

"Oh really? What's that?" he said, his back to me as he placed some of my grandmother's gilded china on an upper shelf.

"Height, Toban. This box was packed by someone who could only reach the bottom shelves."

I swear I could see his shoulders shaking with laughter.

"It seems like you got some help when I was gone, husband," I observed, keeping my voice neutral. "Did the neighborhood children help you pack?" I could picture them now, going through my bathroom cupboards. Finding everything I have ever used. *Lord, save us all.*

Toban turned around to see my flat-faced horror, burst out laughing, and was partway through explaining how it was fine because he paid all the children back in McDonald's, when I decided it was best to take a slow and contemplative tour of the backyard by myself. Maybe I could spot my best friend's apartment from there—or at least find a place to hide until she showed up with the next carload of relics from my turn-of-the-millennium scrapbooking era.

We didn't have much time left to linger. As soon as she arrived and we emptied her car, we piled back into the truck for another round, the day dissolving into a blur of boxes, traffic lights, and me checking my daily step count. By the time the last lamp was wedged into the back seat and the sun had slipped behind the rooftops, I had imagined we would pause for a final look around, maybe say something meaningful to mark the end of fifteen years. But Zach, already drooping, teetered on the edge of tears at the mention of leaving, and Toban was so exhausted he could barely string a sentence together. In the end, we just locked the old door, tossed our overnight bags into the car, and slept over on the Best Friend's ancient futons. The goodbye I had pictured never materialized; the house was empty, and so were we. And it was simply over.

· · ·

She woke me up early, too early, with a little shake and a thermos of coffee.

"Get up," she hissed. She dangled a set of keys pitilessly in front of my bleary face. I glanced over at the sleeping forms of the boys, Zach with his hand pressed hot against his cheek, Toban utterly dead to the world. "Let's go!" she whispered, louder this time. "Don't forget the house keys have to be back with the Realtor by noon."

I wanted to ignore her and put a pillow over my head, but truly there are no words more delicious to a woman's ears than the phrase "don't forget . . ." uttered by *someone else* taking responsibility for *your* life.

Ten minutes, a splash of cold water, and a protein bar later, we were in her car, motoring down the highway, the windows cracked to feel the cool of the morning air.

"Did you hear from him overnight?" I asked, keeping my eyes on the tree line, but I suppose I already knew the answer.

"Do you remember . . ." she began, gripping the steering wheel a little tighter, but then she trailed off. She took a long breath, checked the mirror, and seemed to steady herself for a moment. "Do you remember when he told me to stop worrying that he would leave? He said, 'Imagine that we're kids again. I'm pedaling around on my Big Wheel, making these big loops, but I'm always coming back. I'm *always* coming back.'"

"I remember that, hon," I said softly.

"Well, it gave me an idea," she said, louder now, pulling her car onto the gravel shoulder of the highway with such sudden determination that I grabbed the side handle of the vehicle. She stepped on the brakes and, *whoosh, whoosh,* the sounds of cars racing past sent vibrations running through us.

"Easy, girl!" I said, surprised, but she was already craning her neck around to check the road. She swung open her car door and slammed it. I spun around only fast enough to see her open the trunk, pull something out, and tromp off into the trees beside the road. *What in the H-E-double-hockey-sticks?*

It had rained overnight, and the water glistening on the tall grasses bowed low into a trail where she had disappeared into the woods. You never know the full measure of a person until they up and surprise you, and I *was* surprised. She was gone a good five minutes, and when she reappeared I saw that she was wearing heavy gloves. In one hand she carried a bucket full of different branches and in the other the long end of a pair of super-duty pruning shears. She dumped both in the trunk and swung back into the driver's seat without explanation, and even though I only had a guess about where we were going, something in me kept my piehole shut for once.

It felt strange to see my old house so dark and still. It was always lit up like a jack-o'-lantern. Either because we were too lazy to close the blinds or because nothing terribly salacious was happening, our little bungalow was a neighborhood theater on full display.

She fished in the center console for tissues, grabbed the bucket out of the trunk, and fiddled with the lock until the side door swung open. The place looked odd, bare like that, and I felt a draft of cold air. But then, everything was still.

The house opened into the kitchen, and it felt only natural to see the Best Friend walk to the sink where she had been a hundred times before. She filled the bucket with water and set it heavily down on the floor, water sloshing over the edge just a little, and I resisted the urge to clean it up. Every tea towel drawer was already empty. She turned to me, her eyes full of characteristic earnestness.

"We're going to bless this house," she said. "We're going to bless the crap out of it."

I barked a laugh. Wow. She really knew me.

I wrote a book called *Blessed* about a decade ago. It is a history of how America became fixated on the idea that faith could unlock their health, wealth, and happiness. #Blessed is one of those enduring American theories about what makes someone successful, enviable, and whole. A blessed person conquers difficult circumstances, masters emotions, and overcomes obstacles. She expresses gratitude to others (thanks, ladies!) but secretly believes that everything she got, she earned. I wrote it before the rise of social media, before anyone would even dream of posting a barely there bikini shot with a wink emoji and #blessed. A family in matching plaid sitting on the same tree branch for a Christmas card photo shoot? Definitely #blessed. Anyone without a shot in hell at perfection? *Sorry, Susan.*

But so often, we are not #blessed. Instead, we need a blessing.

It took me a second to piece together what any of this had to do with pruning shears, work gloves, and the mop of longleaf pine branches in my best friend's hands. Then she handed me one, still wet from the trees. We dipped the branches into the bucket a few inches deep with water. We lit a candle she had pulled out of her pocket, and she placed the box of tissues in the middle of the cold marble counter.

For a minute, we just stood there, the only sound a drip of water from the pine needles, letting the weight of it all settle in the empty kitchen.

"Now tell me about the kitchen. What happened here?" she said.

I looked around and suddenly it was as if I were seeing it for the first time. Toban and I had moved from Canada and with "foreign credit" (which is to say, credit that is not imagined to be real), and we were living week to week. But it was in the cowboy days of subprime mortgages and a bank was dumb enough to give me, *a graduate student in religion,* enough money to purchase a bungalow. What a privilege. What a circus. This was the kitchen where we basically got scurvy because we couldn't afford enough fruits or vegetables and all the skin on my husband's hands inexplicably peeled off. This sink was where I bathed my only dog, a ball of cocaine energy and pillowy softness named Huey. Then it was where I bathed my only child, who also seemed to have dabbled with cocaine after sundown. Here I laid dozens of cakes on these counters for birthdays, anniversaries, and gingerbread-house-making competitions where only people who built me a Christmas megachurch were allowed to win.

"This was where I yelled at my father-in-law for the first time for taking a chain saw through this kitchen wall without first putting away any of my clean dishes," I said, showing her where the walls used to be. "But he wouldn't stop laughing or chainsawing."

We traded stories like that, like the time some friends helped me build an eleven-foot wreath that was entirely unsound and we all had to hold up a piece of it for the thirty seconds it remained intact.

"Are you ready?" she asked, taking out the balsam fir branch from the bucket.

"Sure," I said, reaching for mine.

"For the times that this place fed us and didn't. For the times it was filled with laughter and when it wasn't. For all the dishes washed and babies too, bless it all," she said, which was a prayer. And we shook out the pine needles like wet dogs.

Bless it all.

"Next!" she yelled mercilessly.

Soon we were standing where the second floor used to be, where Toban and his father had built an entirely not-to-code staircase that led to an attic that we declared to be a "loft," where more makeshift plumbing was cobbled together. Having grown up in a home where closet doors inexplicably come off and are never replaced, I fell in love with the busy-bee feeling of a family who works together. We could have successfully filmed a home renovation show about two people who can only spend ten dollars a week on improvements but who really don't mind the life lessons learned from getting retinal damage and carpal tunnel syndrome from the same nail gun.

"For becoming someone so very new, so unlike who I thought I could be," I said, shaking my branch all over the stairs.

Bless it all.

We took a few steps until we were standing outside of the bathroom, and a long silence followed. This was where I used to keep most of my medical supplies, the Band-Aids, the gauze, the needles. This is where I would peel off my own surgical tape across my abdomen and clean the clotted edges of fresh wounds with a Q-tip. This is where I wanted to feel confident and beautiful and complete, but instead I was threadbare.

The Best Friend put her arms around me then, the soft rhythm of her breath steady as a heartbeat. She nodded toward the nearby space where the couch had been.

"This is where you used to lie for weeks because you were too weak to even crawl up the stairs," she said. "And Toban bought you those grippy socks, remember? So you wouldn't fall?"

I didn't want to look at her then. This was the place where I used to read plastic-coated books to my fat toddler and his boats, and I learned to successfully replace a leaking toilet seal. This is where I could barely look in the mirror to see a face so swollen from chemotherapy steroids that it was impossible to imagine, even though I didn't need to imagine.

I know what Madeleine L'Engle would say about a moment like this. She once wrote, "We must bless without wanting to manipulate. Without insisting that everything be straightened out right now. Without insisting that our truth be known." It begins with a turning over to love—God's love and everyone else's—all that cannot be altered.

This blessing cannot solve me.
This blessing cannot change the outcome.
This blessing cannot lie about what has happened here.

But perhaps, like my friend Reverend Sam Wells told me in a moment of my great sadness: "If you can't make it happy, make it beautiful."

Yes, this was the place where the previous owner had carefully installed bright green mini-golf carpet all the way from the front door, down the hall, and into an entire Elvis Presley tribute room. This is where Zach roared around in a lion costume for a month and where significant others abdicated caregiving during important medical moments such that I barely had a caregiver at all. This is where we danced to Frank Sinatra after dinner and cried real tears about the end of *Downton Abbey*. And this is where I accidentally sold so many of our belongings in a maniacal fit of being helpful ("Don't worry! You won't want these if I die!") until Toban had to buy back a considerable amount of his office furniture on Facebook Marketplace.

Bless these days. These beautiful, terrible days.

The Best Friend was squeezing really tightly now as I began to shake.

"Damn your terrible foreknowledge in bringing tissues!" I cried, before I burned my way through half the box.

"Should we bless the absolute nightmare of this part of the story?" she asked gently. Which was a fair question. What were we going to do about the worst truths of all?

A blessing cannot say: *this is fantastic, this is great, change nothing.* As the scholar Stephen Chapman wrote, blessing is an act of "emplacement." *This goes here, that goes here.* We can begin to put this moment, or any moment, in the larger order of things. The good and the bad.

When we say "bless this," we are saying: *may everything be put in the right place.* Spiritually, emotionally, psychologically. *Let it be what it should be.*

In these moments, I imagine God as an overzealous interior designer. This lamp belongs in the corner! This awful story about your cancer should only take up the room of that velvet chair! But as we move things around the room, perhaps we might say: *this is not always happy. But perhaps there is beauty . . . there* was *beauty, everywhere.*

"For all the pieces still unfinished, the wounds never fully healed, the scars that still ache. For the love that was and wasn't. *Bless it all.*"

It was almost lunchtime before every wall had been doused with a light mist and every story that absolutely needed to be told had surfaced. And we lay, spent, on the hardwood floor in the large square outline where the couch had been and where the sun had blanched the rest of the room.

"Sorry, love," I said, staring at the ceiling. "I felt like you were trying to tell me in the car about the Big Wheel and about how he would always come back. But then you got the pruning shears?"

She chuckled. "Yeah . . . no, I was just thinking—he will never really be there for me, and he's never really gone. And I deserved a better goodbye. And so do you."

I looked around. The rooms looked bigger, more spacious somehow. I reached for her hand, my palm as clammy as ever.

"Okay," I said. "Bless this heart that's been mowed over. May everything good find its way back; and may everything bad get lost forever."

She squeezed my hand. "Amen."

We stood up, left the keys on the counter, and stepped out, blinking, into a more beautiful day. *Bless it all.*

24

Friend-Tested Rituals for Processing the Everythingness of Life: A List

STEP RIGHT UP! Bonus Games for People Who Want to Stop Feeling Stuck: Choose from among the following activities to see if you can dislodge your own everythingness. Then come tell me about it.

1. This Is a Big Deal to Me Party

You got a promotion! You started menopause! You paid off a loan! You finally switched therapists! You had the hard conversation! Bring a thing that matters to you, and the people who show up agree to make a big fuss about it.

2. The Lunch to Remember

On the anniversary of the death of someone you miss (or maybe on their birthday), have a meal in their honor. Or go to their favorite restaurant (no dishes). Share stories about them and what you wish they were here for this year. Then put it on the calendar for next year.

3. The Body You Have

After a surgery, illness, a milestone birthday, or postpartum recovery, hold a blessing ritual like this: (1) Light a smelly candle. (2) Anoint your scar or stretch mark or wrinkle with oil. (3) Say aloud what your body has carried. (4) Take a moment to bless the staying alive.

4. The Hello and Goodbye

Moving? Make a bucket list for the city you are leaving or for the city you are moving to. Invite friends new and old to check off the restaurants, sites, City's Bests, and re-walk old memories with you.

5. The Terrible Holiday

When our loved ones leave us, we may not know what traditions to hold on to and what to let go. Maybe this year hang their stocking anyway. Or make the weird turnip dish they insisted on (but no one actually liked). Put a seat at the table for them. Remember even though it hurts.

6. For Me? Too Bad!

Your birthday but make it about everyone else. It can be hard to let yourself be celebrated. Instead, host a special celebration on your birthday and honor the people who showed up for you this past year.

7. Hold a Roast for What's Missing

Is something missing? A body part? A person who left *like the fool that they are*? Invite friends over to have a good-natured ridicule for that specific thing or person. Be it your boobs (They were always a little lopsided!), an appendix (Who needs you, anyway!), or the person who made a lot of vows to you (Did anyone ever notice how weird he sneezed?), let everyone make a couple rounds of dumb jokes about why you're better off now. Laugh until it hurts, or, rather, laugh while it still hurts.

8. Happy Anniversary Friendship!

Anniversaries aren't just for romantic partners. Mark the day you met your friend for the first time. Dress up for a fancy dinner, have a slumber party, or re-create your first interaction. Celebrate the people you couldn't live without.

9. Tiny Funerals

Plan a service for something you are grieving—an imagined future, a divorce or bad breakup, or your bad knees that don't let you run like you used to. Write down what is gone on a small card. Light a candle. Wear black, or a shirt that you can tear in half. Read a poem, play a song, or say a simple prayer. Let yourself mark what has happened even if no one else noticed.

10. Festival of Humiliations

Did you get a bad review? Did you get caught doing something embarrassing? Invite friends to read (or reenact) their humiliations out loud with you. Maybe in an accent or in a very commanding voice. Take the sting out of the fact that people out there hate you and are trash-talking you at this very moment.

11. New Year, Same Me

Instead of being frustrated that we will never be new people in January, write a letter of love to the people in your life who make you, *you*. It's never too early to tell people what they mean to you, but it can be too late.

(MOURNING = the ACHe + RiTual)

25

Prescription from Henry

THE PSYCHOLOGIST'S OFFICE was tidy enough, but a man nearing retirement always has a hard time hiding it. The bookshelf was overstuffed with worn paperbacks about the new science of cognitive behavioral therapy and the thick tapestries decorating the walls could have used a good shake. But it was comforting, all of it, because he gave you the sense that it couldn't be otherwise. The beige loveseat where I always sat. The blue armchair where he perched across from me. The concerned lines on his face when he asked me how I was doing this week. Henry was the sort of person you could fold yourself into.

"I know this is our last session," I began, shifting in my chair. "And now you're telling me to piss off."

He laughed first, which pleased me.

"I won't be happy for you," I continued. "Because that would be magnanimous of me. But if I were happy for you, I would say, 'Congratulations on your retirement.'"

"Thank you. I accept your reluctant support," he said, leaning back in his armchair. "It feels very strange to be this old." And we both exhaled in what was probably a truce.

"You're going to need a lot of plans," I said, because cognitive behavioral psychologists love talking about behavior.

"I will," he said.

"Plans you could share . . ."

"I could," he said, maddeningly.

"Plans you *will* share because this is our last session and, what the hell, right?"

He chuckled. "Well, if you must know, I have decided to focus on theatrical monologues. It's good for the memory. It can only be done bit by bit, which gives me a task every day. And I can create a long-term goal of giving a whole one-man show for my friends."

"Wow. That's wonderful," I said, attempting to hide my surprise. Having worked with professors all my life, I can usually spot someone prone to monologuing. But here he was, my most devoted listener, preparing for speechmaking to become one of those kinds of small projects that make a life a good one.

We sat in pleasing silence for a while, thinking about him on a distant planet called retirement.

"I wish I knew what *I* was supposed to be doing next . . ."

"Is there something you'd like to stop doing first?" he asked. He was good like that, keeping his voice low and even, offering these little invitations.

"I can't help but feel like there's a way of being in the world that I've lost. Everything feels like a slog," I said.

He put his pen down, and looked knowingly at me. "These

last few years have been a hard road." And it was as if he said, *consider what you have endured:* cancer, more cancer, less cancer, chronic pain, relationship stress, work stress, and on and on.

"I'm trying to mourn—a friend told me that the best way to live with the ache is to grieve it. But . . . I don't know . . . I wish I could find a new way to feel less burdened," I said. Less weary. Less achy.

Henry wrote something down on his pad of legal paper, which was also irritating. Psychologists are always writing things down about you and the worst possibility would be that they actually read it later.

"Are you writing me a prescription?" I asked, trying to be as annoying as possible.

"Should I?" he asked.

"Absolutely. I mean, we're almost done. Time to let loose some of those opinions stored up under that placid exterior."

He smiled and wrote something down, then he tore off the paper from the bottom of the pad and handed it to me.

It read: *All the joy in the world.*

I held it in both hands for a long while.

"Thank you," I said, quietly. "That was . . . it has been . . . you are a gift."

When the time had come, we stood and lingered at the door, and I gave him a hug because it was the last meeting and who could stop me?

I stepped out of his office and was already partway down the hallway before I suddenly turned around.

"Wait!" I called back. "What would bring you joy? What do you need a prescription for?"

"LSD," he said, closing the door to his office. And the last thing I saw was his Cheshire Cat grin and the last thing he heard was the sound of me choking on surprise as it echoed down the hall.

PART III

Joy

26

A Few Quick Questions Before I Fill a Prescription for Joy

1. I have a thirty-minute window between teaching my last class and a school pickup next Tuesday. Can I collect my prescription sometime around then? That would be more convenient. Please and thank you very much.

2. I half expected joy would happen to me more often since I feel pretty on the up and up with God. Is there something wrong with me? Don't answer that, Kate.

3. A bird once landed on my finger, and I did not feel like Snow White. I also thought about how many commitments I could get out of if I contracted bird flu. What does that say about my capacity for joy? Don't answer that either.

4. The most joyful thing I can imagine lately is a superyacht that sails me away from faculty meetings. After I apologize to Greta Thunberg, who can help me locate one?

I'm willing to lie about my age if it involves Leonardo DiCaprio.

5. According to some rough calculations, bad things keep happening to me at a statistically higher rate than other people. I'm right, right? That doesn't seem entirely *fair*. Is there some kind of math that allows me to receive more joy than other people? I'm looking for some kind of very specific and lucrative divine deal that guarantees some pretty immediate advantages—unless that makes me seem like a terrible person.

27

Ta-da!

ALL THE JOY *in the world.* I feel the weight of Henry's words settle. What *precisely* was I supposed to do now—drive to the nearest Walgreens and ask for a refill of legal euphoria?

Joy had always seemed like something that happened to other people, or to me by accident, if at all. It's a slippery thing. So often when it finds us, it doesn't make any sense. I thought back on the last time joy was there when I hadn't even tried.

Once, many medical procedures ago, I was in the hospital. I will never get used to toggling through so many kinds of fear—emotional, physical, financial. The surgery had been long and grueling, and the recovery promised to be more of the same. And I had already spent down most of my savings on cancer itself—prescriptions, more prescriptions, hospital bills, travel-to-more-hospital bills, physical therapy, and more physical therapists (all introducing themselves as a former athlete named Trevor or Kyle or Brad). Now that the surgery and a stint in intensive care were over, all I wanted to do was go home and eat my own crackers and cry in my own room with the white noise on. Joy was the last thing on my mind.

The sun was pouring in through the blinds, casting ribbed shadows over my bed where I had been anchored. It had been two days since my liver resection. The whole thing had been a bit of a Goldilocks predicament. There had been cancer in my colon and strewn across my liver, but if the surgeons resected too much liver—trouble. But resecting too little—also trouble.

I was so busy looking out the window, wishing to be transported out there, that I didn't notice the surgical resident standing at the door of my hospital room.

"Knock, knock," he said, and my heart sank. *Him* again.

"Knocking is not a metaphor," I said tersely. "That's something you can do. You're right there next to a door."

"Ahhh," he said, his voice decidedly neutral. I made an effort not to look over at him.

I have known healthcare systems only as a maze, one most of us will wander lost and blind. And all the moments of misdirection and misdiagnosis that had brought me to that surgery, in that bed, in that circumstance, had left me with very little confidence that these doctors would treat me as a person whose entire future depended on their willingness to listen.

But then I heard the rapping sounds: *Knock Knock*.

"You can come in," I sighed, suddenly feeling too tired to be annoyed. Earlier that day he had stood idly by as two of his supervisees in white coats ripped off one of my bandages badly, tearing bright red strips across my stomach.

He approached the side of my bed, gathering his expression in a considered manner.

"I'm here to remove the tube in your stomach," he said calmly.

"What?!" I said, but my voice came out like more of a squeak.

The air pockets in the mattress bowed as I scrambled to prop myself up. But there is no scrambling after abdominal surgery. "There is a *tube* in my stomach? That you can remove . . ."

I looked around the room. The flowers in the vase. The television turned to daytime power suits. The unopened peanut butter crackers on the nightstand. I had been waiting for this final check to get the all clear to go home. Someone was on their way to pick me up with a bag of fresh clothes.

"You can remove a tube in my stomach here . . . in this room?"

The surgical resident stared back at me.

I glowered. "Maybe you should start with, 'Kate, you have a removable tube in your stomach.'"

He paused for a moment, looking past me and out the window. Deciding.

He cleared his throat. "Can I start over?"

That startled me. Not soon enough to stop me from rolling my eyes, which I did, but I took a deep breath and allowed myself to take him in. He looked younger than he had this morning, with serious brown eyes and taut lines around his mouth.

"Okay," I said. "But . . . I'd like you to walk in again."

I watched a few different emotions wash over his face in a split second before he nodded curtly.

Then he turned on his heel and strode away.

The monitor beeped like a metronome. The inflatable bed inhaled and exhaled slowly. A minute went by. And then another.

"Knock knock," he said, out of view.

"Come in," I said, a little primly. For decorum's sake.

He walked to the sink in the corner and washed his hands, then strode over to exactly the place he had stood a moment earlier. His elbows were bent, his hands in the air. He looked serious and formidable.

"Kate," he said solemnly, "you have a tube in your stomach and I have to take it out now."

I leaned back in the bed and settled in a little, taking my time. "Why are you holding your hands like that?"

"Like what?"

"Like you are about to do a magic trick?"

"They are clean so I have to hold them like this."

I thought about that for a moment. Then I looked at my stomach, thick with gauze. I hadn't even seen what was underneath. I shuddered. Suddenly there was a long way to go between this hospital bed and my own. I thought about protesting again but was struck by a better idea.

I used to have a brother-in-law who drove trucks for a shipping company, and he was absolutely enormous. He was a competitive bodybuilder who was always standing at the grill in a stringy tank top lecturing me on protein content and describing his latest obsession. I will never forget the weekend I spent at his place recovering from my wisdom teeth removal listening to his newfound love of the magical arts and letting him practice pulling quarters out of my ears with his enormous sausage fingers. What is up his sleeve? Nothing. He didn't *have* sleeves. But meanwhile, back to the hospital.

"I think I would feel better if you pretended to do a magic trick," I told the surgical resident abruptly.

"Um . . . Okay . . ."

He stared at me, uncomprehending, and I stared back at him, a plastic smile now fixed on my face.

His mouth turned flat into a grimace. Or a suppressed smile? I couldn't tell.

"You want me to go out again and come back in," he said. And without waiting for an answer, he spun around and was gone. He didn't pretend to knock this time but barged right in.

"KNOCK KNOCK! YOU HAVE A TUBE IN YOUR STOMACH! AND I AM ABOUT TO DO A MAGIC TRICK," he said in one loud whoosh of a breath, his arms still in the air.

He watched me for a moment. *Your move,* he seemed to be saying. And I had to silently admit that his stubborn commitment to his role and the bolt-upright hands were the bit that did me in.

I obligingly moved to the edge of the bed and pulled down the blanket. Silently we arranged and rearranged my hospital gown to leave my stomach exposed. He put on a pair of surgical gloves and carefully peeled off the thick gauze, pulling back the tape leaving my thin skin red but not torn. Then he touched the skin around the long incision itself, purple and puckered by a dozen staples biting into the flesh, and a fresh wave of pain washed over me.

In a calm voice he said, "I'm going to have to yank really hard, so you will feel a deep pinch, and then a *strong* pull."

I closed my eyes. These were the moments when I could not pretend to be okay—who can pretend away a body?—and I reached out a hand to grip the rail affixed to the bed to steady myself. And then I felt it—the deep pinch—then the strangest wrenching from deep inside, like an anchor wrested from the seafloor. Then the silence of nothing at all.

I opened my eyes.

The surgical resident was standing stock still. Across his white, white coat was a bright spray of fresh blood. And, in his hands, he struggled to hold what looked to me to be two hundred million feet of tubing.

His cheek twitched. He tried to use the back of his gloved hand to wipe what turned out to be another few drops of blood but it smeared.

We looked at each other in horror.

"Ta-da!" he said weakly.

• • •

It did not add up, that bonus feeling that kept me afloat for an entire week. It bubbled up from somewhere in my gut in an area that might recently have been tubing. My eyes started widening, then a light hysteria rising, and then laughter. So much laughter. *His face.* Oh my gosh, *the blood*. Everywhere I looked were alcohol swabs and medication timers and concerned expressions, but here was a gift handed to me out of nowhere.

There had been a small window there, only the tiniest opportunity for anything different to happen. What was going to happen was pain and fear and a surprising removal of a demonic surgical drain. And later I would have told someone in the car, "It was awful. The whole thing was terrible."

But, instead, I felt a stirring. It was almost like something else was nearby and I needed to let it in. And when I did, I was not alone. The doctor—that poor, sweet man—could have said no, but he didn't. He said yes. And then, even though my guts seemed to unspool in his hands like spaghetti, something magical occurred: I felt temporarily and mysteriously whole.

Somehow we had entertained a stranger named joy.

This has happened before, once or twice. Like the moment I looked into my son's enormous pumpkin face and I realized that my heart must have been surgically transplanted somewhere in the process of labor and delivery. It was like I'd caught joy, like grabbing the tail end of a hot-air balloon and being pulled into the sky. Without fear of my grip slipping down the rope until I couldn't hold on at all. Without staring down at the blurry patches of ground suddenly far below my feet.

No, joy was the sharp inhalation of so much gladness in one big gulp that I simply floated away.

Other times it steals in with the dusk and the loons. Joy might even make a sudden appearance at a funeral, and you could almost hate yourself for that surge of helium love you feel as it washes over you.

But most of the time, it exists in the clouds, so far away from where we crawl the earth with our crowded minds, our aching hearts, and our lead feet.

We cannot fix the people we love and, hell, we can't even fix ourselves. The concreteness of every day feels cold to the touch. Immovable by something as fleeting and as useless as an emotion.

But joy.

Brief.

Technicolor.

Like fireworks in the dark expanse of deep, cold space.

But it's been a long time now since I've seen any fireworks. So is joy still for me? Does it only pay a visit when life is so extraordinarily surreal—a surgery, a funeral, a baby?

I keep hoping that somewhere between the grocery run and the emails, I'll stumble into a flash of it, but most days the ordinary feels too dense, too scheduled, too heavy to let anything light slip through. So how do you let in the "ta-da!" when you can barely keep up with the to-do?

The last few years have been such a toggling between the grind and ordinary time. But now, tucked between errands and obligations, is this strange new assignment: to invite more joy into my days, to wait to see how more moments might offer up their own unexpected applause.

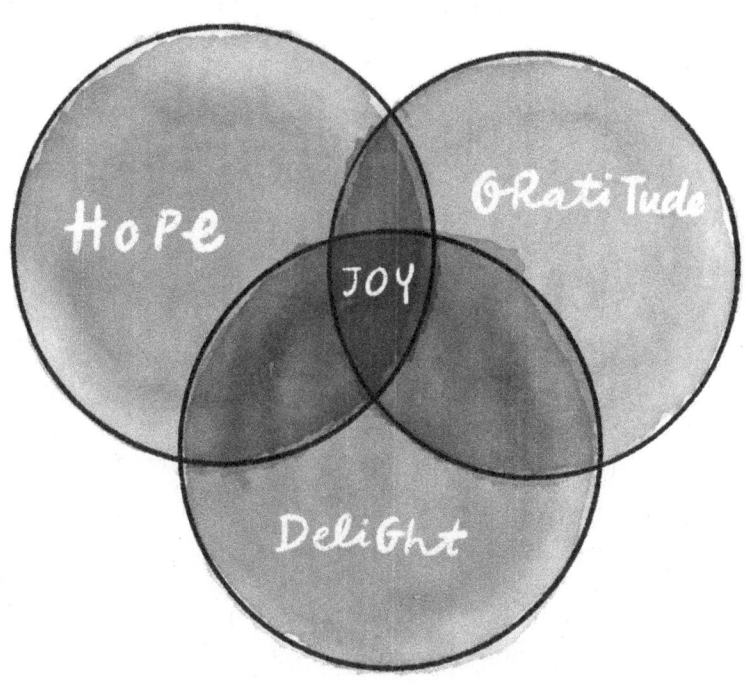

28

Joy (According to Researchers)

1. Joy is uncontrollable. It ranks lowest out of emotions in its ability to be yanked into your life by sheer force of will.

2. Joy is not the same thing as gratitude, exactly, but grateful people are more likely to experience it. And it will make you grateful in the end.

3. Joy is random. You can get used to happiness (see also: hedonic treadmill), but you can't get used to joy. Because you can't get used to a surprise.

4. Joy might be random, but it doesn't mean we can't be more prepared. Theologian Karl Barth wrote that we should hold ourselves "in readiness for joy." On your mark . . . get set . . . joy.

5. You can *almost* make joy a character trait. Not quite, because joy is not permanent. But you can become a more and more joyful person. Wouldn't that be lovely?

6. Joy will make us hopeful. A joyful person will have the ability to see possibilities and grace and even the redemption of things that feel completely ruined.

7. Joy will delight the crap out of us. If you're not delighted, it's not joy. It's probably indigestion.

8. If we want to know if it's joy we should look for feelings of (a) harmony, (b) aliveness, (c) transcendence, and (d) unselfconsciousness.

9. Joy can be easier and easier to experience. We just have to practice.

29

Puzzle Corners

ONE OF THE great, unspoken benefits of being a professor at Duke is that you can wander the hallways nursing a personal crisis under the respectable guise of academic research. One night, I found myself at a faculty dinner, half listening to a colleague from the business school—an expert in behavioral science, an alliance of psychology, economics, and a dash of neuroscience—expound on how even the most unremarkable person can, with the right nudge, transform their life. He described the mechanics of behavioral change with the confidence of someone who has never been ambushed by his own mind at three in the morning.

"I find your science of personal mastery to be exhausting and unlikely," I told him, smiling as I passed him the basket of sourdough. I was becoming increasingly irritated by the number of pumas I had been meeting lately and the likelihood that they were one viral social media post away from their own brand of supplements. He laughed good-naturedly and I remembered, then, that academia is where you stay if you don't believe in totalizing solutions. *God help us.*

"I'm trying to solve a personal problem, and I'm trying not to over-oxygenate my expectations," I admitted, the words coming out more confessionally than I intended.

He set down his fork. "If you want to solve a problem and find the way forward, you have to think about it as a puzzle."

At first, I braced for another formula: a new habit, a sharper morning routine, some clever hack to wedge into the crowded slots of my week. But then he asked, "Who do you want to be?"—and the question landed differently, as if he had shifted the table beneath my plate.

"I'm trying to figure out how to be more joyful," I said.

He leaned in. "When you start a real puzzle, what do you do?"

"I guess I work from the outline, and ideally I start with the corners."

"Exactly. You need to find the corners of what you're hoping for."

He wasn't talking about a checklist or a series of upgrades. He meant something helpfully abstract: that if I could name the boundaries of joy—what it wasn't, where it didn't live—I might begin to see its shape. But what would finding the corners of joy even look like? I knew joy wasn't something I could summon or schedule. It had arrived, unbidden, in hospital rooms and at the edges of grief.

C. S. Lewis once wrote about how confused he felt when he tried to find more joy after experiencing it once or twice.

He would float around from thing to thing as he tried to find the borders: "Is it this you want? Is it this?" *Is this it? Is this it? Is this it?* It sounded familiar.

"What do you do next?" the professor asked, bringing me back to his puzzle. He took his napkin from his lap and pressed the corners of his mouth politely. "You look for the clusters that make sense, the purple that becomes a door, the particular blue of the sky." He said, "So what are some of the groupings that remind you of joy?"

"I have successfully attempted contra dancing?" I offered, uncertain.

"That's wonderful. But are you asking to have more fun? Or is it something else?"

I shook my head. "I know how to have fun . . . I just don't know how to have experiences of joy like I've had in the past." The feeling of being bubble-wrapped in the hospital. The elation of looking into my son's eyes for the first time.

Am I doomed to the same feeling George Eliot wrote about in one of her letters? "Joy and sorrow are both my perpetual companions," she admitted, "but the joy is called Past and the sorrow Present." Where is joy now?

He leaned back, eyes softening. "Then start with the edges. What is going to create the outline of this joy?"

30

Joy (According to the Grief-Stricken)

1. "In the Buddhist tradition, there is a famous phrase that says our lives are filled with ten thousand joys and ten thousand sorrows. Life is filled with an equal measure of both happiness and suffering."

2. "Joy is my late loved one's cat, whom I adopted and who now sleeps with me every night."

3. "Watching a funny show and surprising myself with the kind of laugh that makes me feel like a person again."

4. "Passing around the newest, latest member of the family while in the waiting room. The smiles and comfort that babies bring, even in the very worst situations."

5. "I caught myself laughing today—really laughing. And for a second, it felt strange, like I'd forgotten how."

6. "After everything, my body still knew how to float. I laid back in the pool, felt the water hold me up, and for a moment, I let it."

7. "I saw something that she would have thought was hilarious and went to send it to her, even though. But there is no one to share those inside jokes with anymore."

8. "At the funeral, the pastor mispronounced his name . . . three times. We tried to stay solemn, but in the end we were all shaking with silent laughter. He would've loved it."

9. "The absurdity of spring surprised me again this year. That somehow, after my life has gone to hell, the world still blooms. Doesn't it know?"

31

Trash Walks

It's beautiful in North Carolina in March, which means that Zach has set out to use his metal detector in the woods near our house. He is certain that we are about to embark on a new journey as a family: owning our own junkyard. I tried to explain that a family who owns a junkyard near the woods is actually the premise of a recent bestselling memoir in which the heroine needs to be rescued from her family and taught to read. But to no avail. Yesterday he found a 1936 Chevrolet hubcap and I am done for.

I canvass friends for opinions on whether garbage will add to my quality of life or whether I will simply, you know, incur the wrath of my new neighbors. My friends, being my friends, invariably champion the necessity of objects piling up in my yard. My friend Alex tells me about his friend, a French artist in Russia, whose preferred canvas for paintings is old doors and bits of fencing. In fact, she earned the abiding goodwill of her local Moscow municipal garbage depot after she invited them to her studio and they concluded she was a harmless foreign eccentric and not a trash spy. Such was their friendship that when she left Russia last summer, they invited her to a farewell lunch in the dump. They set up an electric hotpot amidst the piles of trash and recycling, and it was by far her favorite farewell party.

Being Canadian, I am not above a dump party. As a teenager, I discovered that one of the real advantages of working at a rural Bible camp was the privilege of driving the truck to the dump in hopes of holding someone's hand while you watched the bears eat garbage. I even used the occasion to write the chorus of a country music ballad about two people who don't know if what they are feeling is the heat between them or the burning of the trash.

"What's the difference between junk and garbage?" I ask Zach. I have been reading a book by social critic Christopher Lasch about how the endless rush of mass-produced objects makes it harder and harder for us to distinguish reality from fantasy and inevitably blurs the boundaries of the self. In the end, we become our preferences and cannot separate our identities from our coffee orders.

Zach is hunched over a bowl of fruit-adjacent cereal studying a Calvin and Hobbes book lying open on the counter. He looks up momentarily. "Garbage is plastic or cans . . . but junk could be a couch with a lot of cat scratches. You still want to sit on that couch."

"Then how do you decide what to keep?"

He puts down his spoon. "When I dig things up, I am finding something and I keep it for my own collection. So . . . junk is when you find something and give it a new job."

"Like making you happy?"

He looks at me gravely.

"By the way, Calvin has a *saw*." He jabs a finger at the page. I look closer. Indeed, Calvin is cheerfully lobotomizing a snowman.

My son uses this little phrase "by the way" sparingly but effectively when he means to accuse me of something. *By the way, I didn't have my lunch today. By the way, Chris's dad lets him use a knife when they are camping.* By the way, I am filing a formal complaint.

"I don't think a saw is going to make you or me any happier, Zach."

I keep thinking back to the happiness theory known as hedonic adaptation, which posits that people return to a default level of happiness even if something really wonderful (winning the lottery!) or really terrible (lobotomization!) has happened. I feel the truth of it—that I am constantly adjusting too quickly. Did I get a brand-new car? In a week, it's just a car. Did I mostly survive the end of cancer? Now I'm back to worrying about my weight. What could feel like a miracle is a Tuesday again.

"Mom," Zach says, looking at me evaluatively, "when I find a saw, I will keep it under the law of Finders Keepers. Let's go for a walk." By which he meant, *come watch me use the metal detector.*

After sunscreen, backpacks, the detector, and a pocketful of granola bars, we step outside.

"Ahhhhh!" cries Zach, recoiling like a vampire. "The sun is interrupting my face!"

"Dude, this is the whole big thing. You're outside now.

You're supposed to love nature and hobbies and become an adult who talks about birds and tomatoes all the time," I say. I have been feeling very crusty since the pandemic about the whole concept of ordinary pleasures that are supposed to add up to an enriched life. My friend Sarah became a wonderful knitter, her sister mastered watercolors, and the Best Friend would not give it a rest about composting. It was horrible.

"Ahhhh!" he says again, though less apocalyptically. "A dime!"

He bends over to pick a coin from the concrete. He holds it two inches from his eyeballs for a good long minute and then places it in a heavy pocket of his sweater.

"Any trash in there?" I ask, eyeing his jacket, though I know. Once a week I have to stop the dryer because I am laundering too many rocks, and then I give a long speech about bringing too much nature into the house. However, Zach is too pleased to be baited and asks me politely that, from here on out, I refer to his findings as "junk" but not "trash."

I pull out my phone to find a new audience for my complaints.

> Me
> I am on a trash walk with Zach.

> Best Friend
> I love how his joy makes you insane.

> Me
> It's not joy. It's hoarding.

Best Friend

> I'm going to start leaving my garbage bins out for him. Do you think he can fight off the raccoons?

I look up and find that Zach's eyeballs have spotted a distant paper clip glittering in the grass. It is one of the supernatural qualities of children I resent the most: their higher degree of attention. Philosopher William James once described that "curious sense of the whole residual cosmos" as the very definition of spirituality. You don't just live in the world, you behold it.

Perhaps there is a kind of joy that makes you younger and younger. Maybe even though someone tells you when to go to bed and what to eat and what you believe and that saws are reserved for trees and murder, somehow, you feel the unlimitedness—the *anywhereness*—of life's great surprises.

Later that night Zach wants to add his dime to my vast coin collection, which allows him to have all of his pirate treasure feelings while I review the evidence of having been very unpopular in junior high.

Feeling like an especially good mom, I ask him if he wants to get a coin-collecting book so we can put each piece behind a shiny strip of plastic and separate them by country and value. He shakes his head. Some things are better in piles, he explains. Then he runs his toes through his piles before I ask him to stop doing that please. Would he like me to get a coin cleaning and polishing kit so we can examine them more carefully? No thanks. It's better when they look old, he says.

So we have this box of treasure. He pats the box lid like *there, there.*

I keep trying to make these objects into objects, and he resists me. He is too busy filling his pockets with rocks, with his joy.

"How do you know *this* is a joy?" I ask, pulling the tab of an aluminum can out of his jacket before I hang it in the closet.

"Oh, that!" he exclaims. "My Dr Pepper! The best drink of the day!"

C. S. Lewis once wrote that a joy is a joy because it is a reminder. It's not a *this* or a *that,* not a thing to be possessed. Any joy is an arrow back to the heart.

When I look at Zach, trying desperately not to roll my eyes at having to keep *yet another minuscule item deposited in my home,* I realize what an endeavor this would be if I were to follow in his footsteps. Most of the joy I have known has been a kind of escape hatch from pain—a type of joy *despite* circumstances. But this seems to be a quieter species of joy . . . a joy buried inside of the smallest forms of delight.

My son seems to possess a disposition for joy that, coincidentally, I have not seen when he is asked to do laundry. But don't I see children everywhere bursting with the *ability* to be joyful? If I were going to let joy come in through this door, I would have to treat it like homework. Joy would have to be something I accepted as an assignment of gratitude. I would have to learn to respond to everyday graces. Plus, on further reflection, there is probably only one way to conquer the problem of hedonic adaptation: you must rewind the tape and go back to the time when you could be pleased by all the things that cost little or nothing at all.

If you want to be habitually joyful, you have to fill your pockets with ordinary joys.

Zach is in bed with another heavy volume of cartoons and sighs reluctantly as I turn off his bedside lamp. Every night we will review the day, and then we will take turns praying out loud about countries at war and mostly bad dreams. And there, on my knees, I will feel the necessity of this worship at the altar of love.

"Who are you to me?" I ask, pulling the covers up to his chin and kissing his sticky forehead.

We've been watching *Pirates of the Caribbean* again and I still find myself overwhelmed by the same scene of a pirate and his beloved daughter. *Who are you to me?*

"Treasure," he says, and turns to sleep.

32

Joy (According to Kids I Know)

1. "Joy makes everything yellow and happy." *Mara, age 4*
2. "Joy is safe-ing, like Batman when he is safe-ing people." *Henry, age 4*
3. "It's when you feel happy and excited. Like seeing a polar bear and a penguin." *Hana, age 5*
4. "Joy is excitement!" *Juniper, age 6*
5. "When everyone I love is around me!" *Oliver, age 4*
6. "Happiness in your heart that can only come from God." *John, age 9*
7. "Like a bursting feeling!" *Max, age 8*
8. "Balloons and Christmas!" *Shakti, age 5*
9. "Being happy but not, like, circumstantial." *Arabella, age 15*
10. "A real punch in the heart." *Zach, age 11 or 90*

33

Hallelujah

UNLESS YOU ARE incredibly wealthy and can buy tasteful alterations, you get the body you get. And mine requires a few hospital procedures a year to remove things that should not be there and then about ten hours a week of physical therapy, massage, or chiropractic adjustments to stay upright. I am certain I did not start saying "It is what it is . . ." in an old man voice until I developed chronic pain, but *it is what it is*. My older sister says that giving me a back massage is like discovering car parts in bread dough.

When I lie on the adjusting table at my chiropractor's, staring at the water-stained ceiling, I usually have a good long moment to consider the nature of human agency as he cradles my head between his palms, his fingers tuning the vertebrae like the soft hammers of a piano. It is a familiar medical experience, how when it comes to your body, you must mentally prepare to allow things to happen *to you*. You can distract yourself by imagining the side of your pinkie toe pressing against your fourth toe. You can tell your tongue to move in a wide circle around your mouth. But you must not imagine this from above. In a sharp twist to the right and to the left—each velvet popping sound—you must let yourself be *surprised*.

The poet Christian Wiman once said you can't make yourself joyful any more than you can surprise yourself. I'm sure he is right. You can't force a feeling, but perhaps you can make yourself available to it. Maybe you just show up and allow for the possibility that something will shift. You let yourself move, even a little, and trust that something locked up might finally give. The best you can do is hope that, one day, in a moment you can't plan or predict, a sudden rush of lightness will find you—and for a moment, you'll feel free.

I would love a taste of some of that freedom, but the second I imagine it I start to wonder: joy sounds great, but what would I do with my hands?

I don't want to typecast the delightful Mennonite community in which I was raised, but I would venture a guess that no one has ever described us as *free-spirited*. Generous? Yes. Industrious? Absolutely. Handy with a sourdough recipe? Pass the buns, please. Mennonites seem like the last of the Puritans but they are, in fact, long-lost theological cousins to the Amish and a fixture of the Canadian prairies. They are famous for their simplicity, pacifism (with the exception of hockey), and refusal to move with the beat during the good songs at church; I love them with all of my heart for the lethal cheapness that spurs them to fix my roof and mend my clothes, even though I am still getting over the discovery that the nut mix they sent me a few years ago during my chemotherapy treatment was actually expired bear bait.

Looking back I can see that cancer—the helplessness, the uselessness, the ongoingness—made strangers of us all. I spent years in the quiet desperation of a rhythm of scans and treatment, and, without anything to do, my practical family had less and less to offer that would make any concrete difference. It was a long time before my father-in-law, Ken, told me that, after one of my major surgeries, he had been feeling particularly low.

"I made a bit of a bargain," he said, a little sheepishly. "I told God that if you survived five years, I would do the most embarrassing thing I could imagine."

Even that admission made me laugh so hard that we couldn't proceed for a while. I have known Ken Penner since I was fourteen years old, and that man is the king and reigning sovereign of lowered expectations. Every year he gives us a few hundred dollars at Christmas with the warning: "This better not be spent on tattoos!" but I'm convinced he would foot the bill himself if I promised to get LOWER YOUR EXPECTATIONS inked across my back. His philosophy makes complete sense if you are remembering the history of Mennonites as a persecuted people who fled Russia to Canada to seek religious asylum. It makes less sense if you're describing whether your son's killer pickleball team will do well this season. Are things going well? *Life is a series of losses.* It is what it is. When it comes to hope—hope about cancer, hope about anything—my father-in-law is the first to put a hand on your shoulder and tell you, effectively, to stuff any excited feelings you might be having into the bottom drawer.

"Wait a minute! You got your hopes up for me!" I exclaimed to him, more than a little moved. It is easier—it is so much easier—to decide that you will simply wait and see. That you will not be surprised because you never hoped for anything, one way or another. That you will stay as stuck as you were because stuck is *safe*.

It reminds me of a party I went to recently and a friend who is a young widow mentioned that she wanted to date again. The widow's best friend started laughing: "Yeah, right, how are you going to swing that? You avoid everyone! And no one is going to *break into your home and date you, Lucy*!" Which made us all laugh, especially Lucy, and then we brainstormed plumbers, woodworkers, painters, and anyone else she might accidentally fall in love with who was contractually obligated to be in her home.

But isn't that the way it goes? We grow so accustomed to being protective and disappointed that any good thing would need to commit a felony to get to us?

"So what did you promise to do if I survived?" I wondered. My father-in-law has a long and wonderful history of placid responses. No leaping for joy when Mennonites are concerned and dancing is forbidden. We still joke about the moment he was surprised for his twenty-fifth wedding anniversary with a gleaming Gold Wing motorcycle, his absolute dream and a pinch-me moment. He was so overwhelmingly happy. But anyone could see that he didn't feel comfortable being thrilled, and a hundred expressions of concern flitted over his face before eventually someone had to get him a chair because he was going to pass out.

"And *that's* how I handle joy," he chuckled, reminiscing. "So I decided that if you were alive on the five-year anniversary of your diagnosis that I would march to the front of the church and put my hands in the air and shout: HALLELU-JAH!"

Hallelujah. Praise God. Thank you.

Sometime later, when I went looking for scripture passages about joy, I discovered that there are all kinds of shocking divine moments when joy was synonymous with non-sanctioned dancing and nudity. But none of that sounded nearly as embarrassing as the day Ken Penner walked down the carpeted aisle of his church and ascended to the pulpit.

True to his word.

"I'm here to fulfill my end of the bargain," he said to the congregation with a nervous smile.

He confessed that he had been afraid to be hopeful and that he had been deeply discouraged. He told them about the years of uncertainty and how ridiculous it was to think that he was forcing the Almighty to do anything at all. But he wanted them to know that he was grateful, grateful I had lived, grateful enough to be completely out of character.

"This is the most embarrassing thing I could think of," he concluded, grinning.

And then the King of Lowered Expectations put both his hands in the air in a posture of absolute surrender. And he didn't pass out.

Hallelujah.

The congregation cheered and applauded as he stood there like fools do, and rejoiced.

Amen.

34

Sideburns

I WANT IT TO take less and less for me to be joyful. I want to lower the threshold for joy. Wouldn't it be lovely to fall into a foam pit of delight simply because now you are *that kind of person*?

The idea reminded me of a couple I met the other day who loved each other for almost no good reason at all.

It was one of those conference dinners, heavy skirt steaks and speeches where someone begins a toast but then promises to "only say a few words" which devolves into "speaking from the heart" and then, before long, the anecdote machine is pumping out stories at factory speeds. But the couple beside me were having a grand time, hanging all over each other, trading lines of the same story like they have practiced their parts for years.

"How did you meet?" I asked them as another speaker lurched toward the microphone. The woman in the couple had been described to me as quite a shy character, and at first glance I had thought that her face was reserved to display only half-baked expressions of amusement or disapproval. But then she squealed when her husband gave her shoulder a squeeze and I thought, *hold on.*

"Oh! Well!" she exclaimed and scooted her chair to face me.

"A friend thought we should meet," she began. "And I wasn't looking for anyone exactly, but I thought, why not?"

"So I biked over," he continued. He placed his head directly over her shoulder so they were effectively cheek to cheek. "But I was coming straight from a Civil War reenactment. I had changed into shorts, but what are you going to do about this?" He tugged on his mustache.

"It was *enormous*. And sideburns too. Ridiculous sideburns," she added.

"So I biked up and I saw her there. She was wearing a yellow dress." He said it like the closing words of a song.

"I had made it myself," she added, flushing a little at the memory. "I could tell he was looking at me, but that he wasn't sure I was the person he had been set up with. But the *mustache*. His chin was totally shaved so his upper lip and cheeks looked like they had sprouted wings. Actually, it looked like a squirrel had died. I could have just let him keep looking, but then, honestly, I felt like I had to decide at that moment. So I decided and I called out to him."

"Wait," I said, suddenly catching up to the momentousness of what she was saying. "What did you *decide*?"

They smiled at me then, side by side, like conjoined twins.

"That perhaps we would need to take each other as we are. So we did."

And I remembered something that Father Ron had said about delight. "Delight," he said, "is the spontaneous response to the goodness and beauty of life." Outside of children, delight is rare. Unless of course, you decide that mustaches look better as squirrels and yellow is suddenly your favorite color.

35

Microjoys: Tiny Delights People Reported to Me This Week

1. "I'm having a *great* hair day."
2. "My son is home from college tonight."
3. "I made a call I've been putting off for weeks!"
4. "I quit my job because it was toxic to my health. Hard, but good!"
5. "My two dogs love me."
6. "Got to take a meal to a neighbor who had a procedure today."
7. "I took a nap with zero guilt."
8. "We had lemon pound cake for dinner. Nothing else."
9. "I'm terrible, but I love playing my 1972 Yamaha baby grand piano."

10. "My mom's cancer is operable!"

11. "The trees are beautiful out of my window."

12. "The ice cream shop had to kick us out because they were closing and we were giggling."

36

Made for You

"I THINK THAT PICTURING my life getting better makes me uncomfortable," I told the Best Friend over the phone on an early morning walk through my neighborhood. Even though we were only three minutes apart by car we were always still like this, on the phone, constantly on the move. "I mean, sure, that's what I want. But there is an immediate set of secondary feelings that flood me."

"Like what?"

"Like . . . guilt? No, it's less obvious than that. I just feel *weird*."

"You *are* weird about it," she said, but she's a bit out of breath. She has likely finished running wind sprints instead of standing like a normal person waiting for her oil change. You can't tell a woman to calm down. That is a law established before the foundations of the earth were laid. *Do not tell us to calm down.* As comedian Amy Poehler says: "Telling me to relax or smile when I'm angry is like bringing a birthday cake into an ape sanctuary. You're just asking to get your nose and genitals bitten off." But sometimes I wish there were nuclear codes given to close friends for our discretionary use.

"You're one to talk! You are moving through the day at lightning speeds. Your weekend self is your *worst version*."

"No way! *J'accuse!* Think about how awful you are at receiving nice things. Don't get me wrong, you're wonderful at giving presents. But you are truly, unspeakably awful at getting them."

"What?!"

"I can always tell that you're holding something *meant for you* and trying to figure out if you need to give it to someone else," she said. "Like the whole thing with the socks!"

There has been a long tradition on the Mennonite side of my family where you might open a Christmas present that is, say, a bag of tube socks and immediately receive instructions about who else in the family needs to receive a pair from you *immediately* so everyone in the room gets the same amount. A gift isn't a gift until it's been put through a referendum and measured by the Fair-O-Meter.

I shuddered. I had seen the same impulse in so many women who hum with the light anticipation of other people's desires. This hyperattunedness had taken its toll on me and now good things start to feel bad. When I receive a gift, regardless of how much I treasure it, I guess I do have a tendency to start looking around.

"So you're saying that I try to Hot Potato anything good to the nearest person?" I laughed.

"Or you feel like you have to make a nice moment and transform it into a project for all humankind," she proceeded, mercilessly. Geez, she was right. A good thing couldn't just be for me—it had to be *good for all*. Baking? Well, that's obvious. Cookies for the whole neighborhood! Running? I am filling my cup to fill others'. Collecting stamps? I will one day bequeath this to my son. No more examples. I could do this all day.

Otherwise how could I justify sitting around doing something as potentially useless as something that makes me—and only me—truly joyful?

"So if I'm going to accept joy as a gift then . . ."

"Then you'd better get a hell of a lot better at receiving gifts," she finished, pleased to be hammering in the final nail in this argument.

Henri Nouwen, theologian and observer of everyday graces, once wrote that "nothing happens automatically in the spiritual life. Joy does not simply happen to us." It's always been such a rich theological debate about the degree to which any of us can take our faith and transform it into anything concretely good. But I suppose in my heart of hearts I believe that—no matter what—we have to *try*.

This assignment would need some effort.

I thought about the Best Friend's indictment of me all weekend. If joy is a gift, all the best gifts are highly specific. A perfect gift can never be bought in bulk, packaged for mass distribution, and shipped to everyone you've ever met. No, a present is a divine match made between a specific personality and an object wrapped in paper.

There's a kind of emotional arithmetic I keep trying to solve, as if the sum of my happiness must always be divided by the number of people in the room. Maybe I inherited the

Canadian suspicion of surplus—if there's extra, someone must be missing out. But joy, I'm learning, is not a pie to be sliced and distributed until there's nothing left for the baker. Joy is a wild, particular thing, a gift that sometimes lands with a thud right in your lap, and the only assignment is to hold it, awkwardly, as if you're not quite sure whether to pet it or apologize for it.

It reminded me of a massage I had recently when the therapist continued to break the great inviolable Law of Silence by giving sudden and surprising personal insights, like a long explanation of his hobbies. I was irritated until he finished his list: "You can usually find me waterskiing, snowmobiling, ice fishing, or doing burlesque." I twisted my head like a barred owl, eyes unblinking.

"Not normal burlesque," he said, as if that was completely out of the question. "It's *clown* burlesque."

"This makes you happy," I said affirmingly, trying to take the confusion out of my voice.

His elbows were digging into my rhomboid now so I couldn't turn around. I stared at the floor through the face cradle and silently ran through the list of follow-up questions. *Is this a parody? It has to be. Does this reflect the irony of clowns or stripteases? Wait, do they actually strip?*

Suddenly I needed to know if they kept their noses on.

"But it's open to the public?" I asked.

"We sell about a hundred tickets every year. People camp out near Moose Lake, way out near the border with Ontario. A couple dozen tents, always a good time. The first weekend in October."

I shivered. Autumn on the Canadian prairies is a pretty

good dress rehearsal for winter. The trees are already naked and brown, wetted leaves clinging to the cooling earth. Camping? Really? But I could hardly stop myself. If you dangle the words "once in a lifetime" in front of me—no matter whether we are talking about a movie premiere or crippling scurvy—I am going to be *very* interested.

"What if I didn't want to camp but I drove out for the day?" I said, already seeing myself making the trip.

"Well"—he considered—"normally you'd have to buy the tickets in person. But we might let people buy them online for the first time. Do you have crypto?"

I did not.

"Do you have a website?" I asked, suddenly feeling like I needed to check the details before driving for hours out of town to a makeshift camp of stripping clowns.

"We do," he replied, wrapping a hot towel around my face. "On the dark web."

At home, I found myself googling. I found that the going rate for both at-home strippers and clowns is three hundred dollars per hour, and that there was no trace of the hundred or so people on the border of Ontario preparing to see clowns, ambiguously suggestive clowns, tantalizing them with their secrets. Somehow, it always feels very comforting to know that other people are pursuing their absurdities. But let's just say that all I wanted in the whole world was to devote myself to cat magic or hot-dog eating competitions . . . if I figured out how to pay the bills . . . would that be so terrible?

Maybe it's not guilt, exactly, but a kind of survivor's discomfort I'm always batting around. *Why me? Why now?* In the shadow of suffering—my own or the world's—joy feels like a clerical error. Surely someone meant to send this to another address. I want to forward it, repackage it, or at least attach a note: *If found, please redirect to someone more deserving.* But, as I've learned, life does not operate on a merit-based rewards system, no matter how much I wish it did.

I suppose if I assumed a universal joy, available identically to each person, it would be as if I received the most incredible Christmas present, unwrapped it, offered profuse thanks, and immediately handed it to my sister.

If you try to give your joy away willy-nilly, what happens next will likely follow along the same lines as a Christmas Eve I had not too long ago. I had requested a pair of ballooning nightshirts with cartoon dogs. In an act of democratic benevolence, my mother bought them for everyone.

The squeal of my delight upon opening the box was matched only by the long silence of my two sisters.

"Oh, I see," said one.

The other held the enormous billowing pajamas against her body for reference. She looked like a paraglider returned to earth with the sail collapsing around her. She gave a tight smile.

"Look what happened to me," she said.

There was a wonderful and terrible silence as we stared at her flat face.

It was the greatest quip ever made about a gift and, after we wiped away the tears of laughter, we made a solemn vow to resurrect that comment until the end of time.

I need to stop giving everything away and find my own delight. I need to take seriously the fact that I might be the only person on the planet who benefits. How useless, how ridiculous, how wonderful.

Joy is a gift so you can't run around trying to give it away in exactly the shape and form that it came into your hands.

Every good gift and every perfect gift is from above, reminds the book of James. It is for you. The moon and sun, the winter and summer, the birds and lilies—it is for you.

What a treat. It was made for *you*.

Accept it.

37

Among the Trees

I LOVE TO HEAR how people would change. If they wanted to. If they could.

I had a conversation recently with a successful business owner who lived at a breakneck pace under artificial office lights or in the airport waiting for priority boarding. She was long and elegant, and had perfected the effortless luxury of the moneyed class. But with the purple circles under her eyes, the breathless way she spoke, as if she were about to run out of air and time, it struck me that she was probably the most envied unenviable person I had met all year.

"Are you happy like this?" I asked finally. "No, sorry, that's not the right question . . . Let me ask you this instead: what would you do right now if you could?"

She smiled, and pulled out an illustrated book about nature from her Gucci purse and placed it on the table between us. She tapped the cover, and then let her hand rest on it gently.

"I would take my place among the trees."

She said it like you would a prayer. *God, put me back into the order of things. Plant me here.*

And I murmured approval, and I resolved to try, try and take my own place among the trees. Whatever that means.

.   .   .

One of the most unusual parts of living in Durham, North Carolina, is that it is home to the largest concentration of lemurs living outside of the island nation of Madagascar. There are nearly two hundred and fifty of these surprisingly fluffy primates across twelve species, which means that Durham has, by extension, the highest number of lemur-related tattoos and bumper stickers declaring this to be a universally recognized truth: I ♥ LEMURS.

Thinking about all the clown burlesque going on outside of my supervision, I decided to sign up for a weekend at one of the university's research centers so that I can learn about lemur habitats. I've always wanted to do this, but there has always been something more urgent to attend to—and also not a single friend ever wanted to come with me. But now I have been given a prescription for joy, so, yes, sign me up for a walk with lemurs please.

Early on a Saturday morning, I drove down the long gravel road that cut through the trees until the Jurassic Park–style protocols of electric fencing and enclosures began. The forests stretch on and on, and up and up, and no matter how many years I've been here in North Carolina, the trees remain unfamiliar. The enormous oaks are scaly and slate gray, the magnolias are disconcertingly tropical, and the longleaf pines smell nothing like the squat, fragrant evergreens that make the northern prairies of my homeland into an oversized Christmas tree farm.

The researchers and curators who run the lemur program welcomed me and my fellow enthusiasts warmly. The morning was spent watching videos, considering the intricacies of lemur behavior, genomics, physiology, and even paleontology, touching leftover lemur skulls, and really thinking about the gifts that these tree-dwelling primates bring to the world. We learned about their breathing, their feeding patterns, the rings on their tails like the trees they hang from.

It's an age-old story. First comes the establishment of a lemur center and animals are released into a free-range enclosure. Then come the tarsiers, a tiny and hideous mammal, and a number of professors are hired as colony managers for them. Their enormous eyeballs are so horrifying that they can't rotate their heads around them, but their charismatic potential is overwhelming. Soon a hit show is developed for public television called *Zoboomafoo* featuring Jovian, one of the fluffy maroon-and-white lemurs—who survives sixteen episodes of the first season before he is replaced as the star of the show by his own son. The treachery.

"Jovian was going bald," explained the curator, because even lemurs cannot escape the vicissitudes of male-pattern baldness. We can't all be stars.

Lemurs are the single most endangered mammal on earth. The research center buzzes with heroic efforts to move the entire species from being endangered to surviving to reaching optimal levels. But there are few babies born, and some of the other species that the center houses, like the godforsaken tarsiers with the eyeballs, seem unusually predisposed—if disrupted by a loud noise—to bang their own heads against the wall until they end their own lives. Or light. Or people. By noon I'm convinced that if something is so endangered, it should be kept in a dark, silent, isolated, tastefully appointed cage and forced to live there comfortably but, most importantly, safely. Problem solved!

I explain my solution to the curator and wait for her approval.

"Yeah, we could," she said, simultaneously filling a bag of Craisins. "We had a huge debate about that. But the best solution is to create a world in which we duplicate their natural behaviors."

I think back on my Instagram-powered learning about gratitude and breathing. And water. And 11:00 A.M. digestion. Perhaps if we follow a more natural course, we can be returned to our own set point. Maybe that is the pathway to ease suffering and open ourselves up to greater capacity for more of all that is good.

Best Friend

How is the lemur walking going?

Me

They are passing out Craisins to them. Craisins are the fentanyl of the lemur world.

Best Friend

Why Craisins?

> **Me**
>
> No idea. But apparently they will compromise themselves for ten Craisins.

It is Sunday, the second day of lemur immersion, and their behavior is beginning to feel like an explanation. For example, males cannot reach sexual maturity while living with their parents. The impulse is *suppressed,* said the curator pointedly, and the woman beside me who had finished complaining about her adult son at home choked with a surprised laugh. But we decide, as a group, that these are astonishing creatures. They can count to seven! They can recognize complex social hierarchies! They can even move purple, red, and orange paint around a drop cloth and create art for us to take home. This critically endangered species is vital to the future of the world as we have come to understand it.

"But why do so many of the lemurs wear horse blinders?" I wondered, still awash with awe. "You have this beautiful facility with so much room that they can move freely."

Well, apparently recognizing complex social hierarchies has its downsides. Like the fact that a lemur might be consumed with rage for another lemur to the point where he has to wear headgear that prevents him from seeing his nemesis walk the earth.

At a certain point in the day, the moral superiority of lemurs has become entirely out of the question. The sound of lemurs screaming from the cages meant that I was just in time to watch them engage in "stink fights" where, during mating season, male lemurs will rub their scent glands all over their tails and flap them in the air or at one another to establish dominance and reproductive priority. They are chirpy like hockey players after the whistle. The curator called it Trash Talk O'Clock.

Then the lovely little Jane Goodall taking care of the ruffed lemurs informed me that the lemurs frequently slap one another and that slap-fighting was so common that, in fact, *she* had been slapped—so many times she couldn't possibly count.

"JUST REMEMBER SLAPPING IS NORMAL!" she called out when a tiff broke out among two of the lemurs, which sent me into hysterics.

"This is an incredible species," said the adoring crowd. Absolutely incredible.

Best Friend
> Can you be done appreciating lemurs now? I need to talk.

Me
> Did you know lemurs can solve complex puzzles?

Best Friend
> I did not.

Me
> But they can't entirely get Craisins out of a paper bag?

Best Friend
> I'm really starting to understand why they are endangered.

As the event came to a close, we walked back through the forest to the information center where we had first gathered and parked our cars. We headed down a path and, as we turned, we reached a small clearing where the weak light from the April sun settled on a patch of grass. And there was a cluster of ring-tailed lemurs. A troop.

It was startling.

They sat serenely with bums planted, their arms outstretched, bellies hanging forward, and legs folded in front of them. Perfectly still. Like tiny Buddhas.

Yogic sunbathing. Deepest calm.

"May you find ease," repeats a famous loving-kindness meditation. "May you find ease."

I took a deep breath. I could feel my shoulders drop, and I resisted the urge to step out of the shadows and sit down beside them.

"Do you think lemurs experience joy?" I asked one of the animal curators before reaching my car.

She paused, ticking through the evidence in her mind. "Well, we resist the urge to anthropomorphize their experiences as much as possible. So it's hard to know what emotions they have. I certainly see excitement when I bring a bag of painting supplies, because they know they are about to get Craisins."

I had, in fact, experienced zero joy watching lemurs almost accidentally use paint while trying to get Craisins.

"But . . ." She paused. "There is a moment. In the cool of the morning. I can go out to the forest and see them sitting out in the sun. I guess . . . I guess I would say that when they are set up to display their natural behaviors, they seem most themselves."

There are some acts that are so natural. A cat deep in a luxurious stretch. A bird flexing its wings. A troop of lemurs warming their bellies.

I thought back on the exhausted woman trapped under fluorescent lights who wanted to stop conquering the world for a moment and simply live inside of it. Perhaps we all intuit that we cannot simply survive. We will need joy like air, like water, like Craisins.

Some experiences seem to transport us. Swinging in a hammock. Throwing an arm around a friend and squeezing. Feeling someone comb their fingers through your hair. Sleeping and eating and lying in the sun. We feel most intensely ourselves for a brief moment. We take our place among the trees.

38

The Nurse

THE ROOM WAS remarkably quiet. Through the gentle darkness I could make out the outline of the Best Friend sleeping in the corner, her chair reclined into the not-quite-bed position that hospital furniture manufacturers have perfected. She snored softly, face mask over her eyes, the very picture of serenity.

Only hours before she had terrorized the emergency room, supervising the administration of my medication, demanding a second pillow. *Can she get another apple juice? Has someone checked her fluids?* There is no force greater than a best friend, an emergency, and a checklist. And now she had blissfully passed out, my trauma concierge.

The whole situation had been completely out of hand.

We had been on the phone, walking and talking, as we do. A block from my home there is a narrow creek that leads to our neighborhood park. I had stepped off the path by the bridge to make way for a man with his dog, standing on the mown grass for only a moment, when I felt a pinch around my ankle. It was an ant or a mosquito, certainly, so I glanced down but kept walking.

"Blah blah blah," she was saying, which wasn't like her. She's usually a great storyteller.

"Uh-huh," I replied, imagining that I would catch up to whatever we were talking about, eventually. I stopped for a second to pull my sock down a smidge, hoping to see exactly where the ant or mosquito had done its worst, but there was nothing really that I could see. I shrugged and kept walking.

"Blooobedy blah blah," said the Best Friend again. "Are you even listening?!"

"Sorry," I said, "I'm just . . . I'm just limping for some reason."

Anyone who has experienced chronic pain knows that it comes in flavors, but this one was new to me. This pain came in prickly waves, and then it subsided. Another wave, and then receded. It was intense, but not overwhelming. I had certainly felt worse. So I kept walking.

"I was thinking about trying a dating website, but I refuse to fill out the part where . . ."

"I'm not sure I should be limping," I interrupted, when I realized that I was practically hopping at that point, and explained the same thing to my husband when I got home. He rushed to the closet and took out my makeup mirror with the magnifying light and held it up to my ankle. Zach found us staring at my ankle through the reflection for a good long while. Two small puncture wounds lay right above my ankle.

"That's not an ant bite," Toban said, concerned.

"I don't think that's a salamander," said Zach, with earned authority.

"No," I said, wincing. "It's not."

Taking my place among the trees had its disadvantages.

We all piled into the car and within fifteen minutes I was walking into the local urgent care. I hopped up to the desk and reached for the intake form, briefly scanning the room to see how long of a wait it would be. These processes normally take a few hours and so I had brought a book.

"So, I was recently bitten by a snake and . . ." I began.

The woman behind the desk looked up at me, startled, her eyes saucers.

"Ma'am. Did you just tell me that you were BITTEN BY A SNAKE?"

"Yes, but it's not that bad and . . ."

"GET OUT OF HERE!" the administrator yelled. Everyone in the waiting room snapped their necks toward me.

A nurse who had overheard this exchange jumped to her feet: "GET OUT OF HERE YOU'VE BEEN POISONED! TELL THE EMERGENCY ROOM YOU'VE BEEN POISONED!"

"So you want me to . . ."

"GET OUT OF HERE OR I'M CALLING AN AMBULANCE! SCREAM AT THEM IN THE ER IF YOU HAVE TO!"

Another fifteen minutes later I was limp-jogging through the Duke Emergency Room doors, having been there so many times before. When I had cancer that had spread through my abdomen, and the pain was so great I could barely walk, I had been sent home from this exact place with Pepto Bismol. Before I left I told them—I begged them—to admit me to the hospital. I explained to every person I saw that the pain was so unbearable that I couldn't take it much longer. But they sent me home and, for months, the cancer spread.

But today, breezing through the doors with a level of pain I would still describe as "recreational," I felt ready to shine.

"I HAVE BEEN POISONED!" I declared to the security officers manning the metal detectors, who allowed me to pass.

"I HAVE BEEN POISONED!" I yelled to the intake coordinator, my hand on the forms she had asked me to sign, but I just gave a little shake of the head as if to say, *sorry, I've been poisoned.*

Two doctors immediately pulled me into a separate room and crowded around my leg with sophisticated medical instruments: a magnifying glass, a ruler, and a Sharpie. They circled the bite with the Sharpie, used the ruler to measure how far the poison had made its way into my blood system, and, after about an hour, tried to get "The Snake Bite Guy" to call them back.

"It's probably a baby copperhead," said the beefier doctor, who looked like he had chosen between this and the marines. "Spring is the worst time for snakes because the babies are chock-full of poison."

Charming.

"It looks like you've been here before," observed one doctor, who I was silently calling Doogie Howser, M.D., for the look of sweet childlike horror as he scrolled back over an endless list of my past hospital visits. The other, Doctor Tight Sleeves, was trying to get the snake bite consult on the phone, when he also could have been looking for larger scrubs.

"Oh yes," I said pleasantly, "you guys almost murdered me before."

Doctor Tight Sleeves pulled the phone away from his face.

"Just so you are aware, the antivenom is going to be at least one hundred thousand dollars to mix and administer."

I guessed that it was Doogie Howser's first rodeo because he looked even more pale. "Do you have insurance?" he whispered to me, so as not to interrupt the phone conversation.

"I can't wait to find out what you plan on doing if I don't," I said, smiling with venom of my own. Normally I am the Dora the Explorer of hospital intakes, but there was something about having to review the history of their medical neglect in the very room where it had last happened that was pushing me past sadness, way past anger, and into something like surreality.

Doogie was watching me squeeze my eyes tightly as I waited for another wave of pain to pass. It was getting significantly worse.

"That's the poison really getting into your bloodstream," Doogie said, failing to sound nonchalant.

Doctor Tight Sleeves called over again from the phone: "Hey! We'll get that antivenom going in a second, but the pharmacy has to make a batch for you. And, look, chances are good that you'll keep the leg!"

"You'll keep the leg," echoed Doogie, and I pressed my lips together for a moment, squeezed my eyes shut, and tried to will myself to be *anywhere else*.

"But the snake guy says you'll probably need two doses," Doctor Tight Sleeves said loudly.

Cool, cool, cool. Just more than the cost of my home.

For a second I wanted to yell: *I HATE THIS I HATE THIS I HATE EVERYTHING THAT HAPPENS HERE. You ask me to rate my pain on a scale from one to ten, but you don't listen to the answer. You ask my birthday again and again to double-check my identity against your protocols but don't care who I am. You talk over me, past me, and about me, but I will never have enough money to be listened to. You need me to be a professional about all of this, but I am being pulled apart stitch by stitch and you will never put me back together.*

Then I had another thought.

"Do you have to stay here with me while I wait?"

"I do," said Doogie.

"Then until the antivenom arrives and is fully in my bloodstream, I'm going to tell you every single thought that's ever occurred to me about medicine."

And I did. I monologued for hour after hour after hour. I pulled up The List and every instance of medical neglect that had done me wrong. I used names and specifics and details, and if there was a pause I would say: "FEEL FREE TO CHECK MY RECORDS ARE RIGHT THERE." I rode the wave of all this heightened urgency with a feeling of amused calm interrupted by wave after wave of pain. And then, mercifully for all of us, I slept.

• • •

I was in a dark room down the hall, attached to the IV pole, when the nurse came in again to check my fluids, her high ponytail bobbing. She was young, but that doesn't mean much with nurses. They learn hard and fast.

"Hello," she said softly, glancing over at the Best Friend asleep on a chair in the corner. "I'm just going to check a few things. Don't mind me." She clacked away at the computer for a few minutes and scrolled through my chart.

"I've never been in the emergency room overnight," I said. "I'm normally shuttled off somewhere exciting. But this place is buzzy, isn't it?"

"It is. It's very buzzy. I think that's what I like about it."

"I did notice that the people I've already met—that beefy doctor, the intake person—have a certain . . . I don't know. Punchiness? Alertness?" I chuckled.

She smiled as she pulled out the rolling stool and sat down. She took out a roll of medical tape and some scissors, cut a few neat strips, and got to work adjusting and re-taping my IV.

"I saw on your chart that you're a bit of a frequent flier here," she said.

"Yeah, I mean, I've been here in the hospital a lot more than I'd like? Yes, that's true. I hate it. I mean, I *hate it*. But I also feel extremely myself here."

"This place has a way of doing that."

"When I was dying, I was sent home from this emergency room with Pepto Bismol," I said, but too brightly. I am starting to notice how often a strange *nothing to see here* tone of my voice signals that I am about to drop an anvil.

She shook her head and placed the last strip of tape on my hand, gently smoothing the edges.

"My husband died here," she said quietly. She looked up.

"Wait, do you mind if I tell you? Most people don't know. And I don't usually tell patients."

I waited until she made eye contact again, and she twisted her mouth uncomfortably.

"Tell me," I said.

"Well." She cleared her throat. "He died very suddenly. No warning. His heart just . . . stopped." She turned away then and became very interested in the machines. "I've been asking for these overnight shifts because . . ."

"It feels normal."

"Yes. It feels normal."

"Because this is the place where things like that happen? At least that's how I feel. Look at my chart, and it will tell you that I belong here."

"Right. I feel heightened here." She wiggles her fingers as if feeling an energy. "There's a hum to it, the noticing, the alertness."

"Yeah, it's quite the waterslide. The hospital has a way of sucking you in and shooting you out the other side."

She laughed dryly. "That is the best part. Time isn't dragging when I'm working. But then I go home and it's laundry and dinner and the normal, ordinary kid stuff and I feel so . . . tired. I'm exhausted. But not here." She tapped the walls of the room with her fingers. "Here I'm very alive."

"Well, you're very good at taking care of people like me. Look at this IV insertion. I am terrified of needles but this is top-notch," I said.

"I can't tell *what* I'm doing," she demurred. "I came back to work and that's as far as I got. I can't tell how the kids are doing."

"This must be such a surreal experience. How does anyone know how to parent in that situation?"

"Well, we haven't moved anything around or gotten them settled differently."

"Wait, when did this happen?"

"Last month."

"Oh, love . . ." I breathed.

She looked away again, and a long pause settled in. The white light of the oximeter on the monitor flashed my heartbeat in a steady pulse.

It is strange the kinds of truths we can tell in the dark, when we are unsure if this place is the basement in which we are forever locked. We might wonder if we will ever get out, or if we will even try now that we have been here for so long, disciplined into suffering.

"No one is ever going to say this, because it's not the kind of thing people who work in hospitals say." She put her hand on my hand, carefully, and turned so she fully faced me. There was a quality of attention now in the room that felt almost sacred.

"But I guess what I want to say to you is, I'm sorry." She took a breath and I felt my own catch in my throat. "I'm sorry that happened to you and that it happened here and that people should have cared so much more than they did. I really am."

I tried to say something, but the words wouldn't form. Tears sprang to my eyes and dribbled down both my cheeks, and the tightness in my chest felt like it was going to suffocate me until it gave way to deeper, fuller breaths. All these hours—but all these years, really—I had been stuck in these familiar rooms in a Groundhog Day of the same, same, same. Same fear. Same anger. Same worthlessness. Same utter conviction that things would always be the same.

During all those long hours in the emergency room I had descended down, down, down through these memories—this resentment, this fear, this poison—and then, just like that, I felt this burst of joy.

It was a feeling of liftoff. A lightness. A bounce upward and outward as so much unforgiveness fell away.

She had placed her fingers directly on the ache, felt its pulse, and had not pulled away. It was the most incredibly expansive feeling in my chest—like a lead balloon suddenly filled with so much helium that we were carried into the sky.

The man pushing the gurney down the hallway a moment later would have seen a nurse leaning over the bed to take a patient's hand, two strangers staring moonfaced at each other for a long minute working out an invisible sum: how you can be loved into a kind of wholeness.

Anywhere.

You can be complete, for a moment, you really can. The ache simply ceases to matter.

Even with a tube in your arm, poison in your leg, and a fresh widow on the night shift emptying her pockets to pay someone else's debt.

39

Off the Edge

GOOD NEWS: YOU might arrive at the hospital screaming, but after a successful envenomation and antivenomation you're allowed to drive yourself home.

I was ambling to the parking deck after the snake incident when I called my parents in Canada to let them know that, all things considered, I was fine. My parents picked up immediately and put me on speakerphone.

"Speak. Caesar is turned to hear," answered my father, which was typical. He frequently displays the kind of penchant for drama that is likely genetic. Recently, I was putting Zach to bed and as I turned off the lights and whispered, "Good night, sweetie," the words "I WILL HAVE MY REVENGE" followed me out to the hallway.

"Well, your daughter will keep the leg," I said, equally dramatically. "But honestly, I had a weirdly positive experience. It felt very . . . healing."

"Oh, sweetie," fretted my mother. "That's lovely. But we were worried."

"The sheer variety of your possible deaths!" marveled my father. "I will follow your career with interest."

"Actually I did reach out to your shark guy while I was under sedation," I said, piecing together a bit of what had happened during my hospital stay. "So there's still a shark death in my future to consider. But first I'm going to jump off a cliff. Let's allow nature to finish the job!"

I felt myself merging onto a strange mental superhighway. After the nurse—after that incredible feeling of emotional cohesion—I had the overwhelming desire to start thinking about the future. I would make plans! Fun plans! Fear has a wild way of making us alert, wary, and hungry for more life. You feel whisked away from the realm of the ordinary and then it occurs to you that you shouldn't necessarily go back. Didn't my parents know someone who ran a university laboratory to study sharks? Didn't I always want to soar through the sky like an angelic Canadian Goose? Flap flap. I felt certain that I should immediately find out.

Healthcare professionals familiar with the side effects of morphine might recognize an unusual sense of well-being and unearned confidence in their patients who are completely high, but who could have anticipated how quickly one motivated woman can sign up for a lot of dangerous hobbies? It only took about fifteen minutes for me to contact my parents, force them to dig up the email address of a marine biologist they once met on a cruise, message him, discover his typical sailing times, and invite myself along. Easy! We would be taking a party boat out into the coastal waters off of South Carolina and pulling dinosaurs as large as eleven feet and eight hundred pounds out of the water with a limited liability waiver because that man was retiring soon and did not care. I loved him already!

Other great ideas? Paragliding. Definitely paragliding. I was supposed to be on a plane the next day to give a lecture in a lovely mountain town and, in the morning, after the nurse's shift had ended and the doctors were considering administering another batch of antivenom, I may have said, *sorry I'm going to need you to hurry this up. I've decided to jump off a mountain on Tuesday.* And then I got a very helpful lecture on the likelihood of a delayed allergic reaction called "serum sickness" but I would have a lot more time to consider the odds on the first leg of my trip, perhaps somewhere over Kansas.

The heightened urge to feel fully alive did not subside by the time I was in the back of a Jeep headed up the mountain. We were all in this together! Life was for living! The driver threw a couple clipboards in the back seat for me and the other soon-to-be gliders. I gave it a once-over. The form was less of a sign-this-waiver situation and more of an application, but, as I glanced around, the other people in the back seat were already busy filling it out.

PILOT'S NAME:
FLIGHT DATE:
PILOT'S BIRTHDAY:

I hadn't met the pilot yet so I left that blank. I had signed up to be strapped to another living person who would jump at the same time and control most of the sail, *thank you, Jesus*. I looked around. An enormous man with a shaved head appeared to be driving behind the Jeep on an ATV with some others—that was probably him. Moving on, the next section was mostly requiring that the pilot would not sue for losses incurred as a result of injury, death, or property damage. The fact that property damage was listed *after* sudden death as cause for legal concern seemed about right when we took into consideration all the side effects of leaping off of a cliff at a pricey Colorado ski resort.

Conveniently, the rest of the form had already been filled out with a new membership number for a thirty-day temporary license from the US Hang Gliding & Paragliding Association.

"You want me to get my paragliding instructor to sign this?" I shouted a little to be heard over the motor. "Doesn't my instructor already have a license?"

The driver nodded, his eyes on the rough trail ahead and another steep incline.

I persisted: "This is for a provisional license. The guy who is taking me today is a real paraglider, right? He's been doing this for more than thirty days?"

We were fully revving up what appeared to be the final hill, which leveled out into a grassy patch of pasture, and the driver pulled to a sudden halt. He turned around to smile at me.

"That's for you, pilot. Sign at the bottom and congratulations! You've just received a thirty-day provisional license to jump off this mountain." And with that he hopped out.

I felt my stomach drop out of my body for a while, but both legs got out of the car and walked around. I met Tompk, my Estonian instructor, who found me zero percent amusing. He found it even less entertaining when I stopped trying to tell jokes about the pilot's license and started rearranging the sail he had carefully placed on the ground.

"I'm worried that these pieces of grass are going to get stuck in the strings!" I could hear myself saying hysterically, as Tompk strapped the lightweight harness around my body and adjusted all the straps. Why were there so few straps? How many straps does it take to get down the mountain? There were pulleys and leg straps and carabiners and hooks and *holy crap this is just a nylon backpack.*

We were standing eleven thousand feet up, and the path down was obvious. We would have to jump off the top of this cliff and glide thousands of feet to an open field somewhere below. I don't know how I did not actually think about the landing. Do we land in water? On our feet? Are we carried to further safety by benevolent birds?

Tompk stood in front of me now, looking down sternly. I tried to stare past him, but all I could hear were the sounds of other paragliders running toward their own deaths. Footfall and then a shriek. Footfall and then a shriek. Well, I guess that was the end of them. I wanted to let out a sigh, but my heart was in my throat. It must be my turn by now.

"I need you to run," said Tompk in an impossibly low and stern voice. "You will run? Yes. You will run and then nothing will be under your feet but you will run."

I was absolutely silent, unblinking. I could hear the click as he hooked himself into my flimsy death backpack behind me.

"What will you do when you feel nothing?" he repeated.

"I will run?" I muttered, but my brain was somewhere in a pile I left in the Jeep.

"YOU WILL RUN," commanded Tompk. "YOU WILL RUN RIGHT NOW."

"Maybe we go over there and run off that safer ledge!" I was frantically pointing to another imperceptibly different part of the cliff.

"YOU WILL RUN, LADY! YOU WILL RUN NOW!" Tompk yelled and something in my brain jolted into motion. I was running. I was running toward the edge of the grass meeting the sky and then I ran straight past the part where feet are doing anything interesting. Tompk grunted as he slammed into my back.

"Was I supposed to keep running?!" I called out, but the wind was whooshing in my ears. I was expecting a sudden drop but instead the earth seemed to have fallen away from my feet. The green grass was starting to become the tops of trees over the slopes of the mountains. I pressed my back into Tompk a little to feel if he was still there; he was so quiet. The Estonian brick wall did not budge. He felt warm, and as I settled into my first few breaths I began to feel the surrealness move into something else. Was I safe now?

"What was elementary school like in Estonia?" I stammered. I could feel Tompk's whole body sigh, as if he had already met his quotient of lightly hyperventilating women in his lifetime. But, to his credit, he began to monologue in precisely the low and lulling manner that has made many a Sleep Story narrator famous. It all began for him in the 1990s in the Baltic states, followed by a careful account of when he first heard about Michael Jordan and what it would have been like to join the Estonian basketball league. The roaring of the wind in my ears began to quiet as I listened, and my heartbeat slowed long enough for me to notice the green carpet spread out underneath our feet.

The landscape stretched out in sharp, clear detail—evergreens clustered like dark brushstrokes against the lighter patches of aspen and meadow. The valley below moved slowly, calm and steady, as if time itself had paused to watch us pass. Below, the shadow of our sail zigzagged across the valley floor. Above, another paraglider careened across my sight line, laughing.

For the first time all day, my body stopped bracing for disaster. Should Tompk and I get married? That was the only reasonable solution to staying this safe forever. Also, how do we land again?

I'm so grateful that I had no idea that we would skid to earth on our bums like failed water-skiers because I was too scared to land at a jogging pace using my legs. As we slid to an undignified stop in the grass, silence fell, broken only by the sound of nylon scraping across the field and my own surprised cackle. My shoes were full of turf, my elbows tingled, and for a moment I just lay there, blinking up at the sky like someone who had fallen out of a perfectly good airplane. Joy had shown up grinning like an idiot.

And I could not get enough. A week later I was in South Carolina dangling my legs over the side of a research boat before the Shark Expert was like, "Lady, if you don't try harder I can't help you." So I reeled in my limbs, stopped trying to rescue my fifteen-dollar sunglasses that had fallen into the water, and spent a full day luring dinosaurs to the surface with headless chunks of tuna and then tagging them with trackers so we could create a lifelong friendship.

There was something about the insanity of being bitten on a mowed suburban lawn during baby copperhead season that seemed to have dislodged a new response to fear. I didn't realize how intensely guarded I had been—how physically tight and nervous I felt—until I stopped trying to be quite so self-protective. And with more vulnerability came more opportunities—more space—for joy.

Over the next few months I found that all I wanted was to wait for joy like I was standing in traffic. I drove out to the ocean and went kayaking at night on the hunt for those bioluminescent moon jellies. I rented a pirate ship intended for children for the Best Friend's birthday and poured wine for the crew until everyone was willing to learn the lyrics of the sea shanty "Barrett's Privateers." ("I was told we'd cruise the seas for American gold; we'd fire no guns, shed no tears!") I did an entire photo shoot at the World's Largest Praying Hands. I spoke to the sweetest man who transformed a tank of liquid fertilizer into the world's second-largest fire hydrant with some spare paint. In the culture of necessary realism, wouldn't it be better if a bunch of volunteer firefighters in rural Manitoba didn't care one bit if a slightly larger fire hydrant was right down the road?

I started to develop an informal theory about joy's sudden appearances. Most of my days are heavily freighted with routine in order to maximize efficiency (see also: human woman) so I am unlikely to be surprised by anything except what adds to my mental load. The sameness—the sameness—the sameness. Essentially, like the avoidant widow, anything good would have to break into my home. If I wanted to discover *anything* lovely, I would probably have to start by allowing myself to find some off-ramps, some byways, some cliffs.

When we stand in the way of joy, she appears. Not joy in general. *Joy for you.*

I called my parents again in the glowy aftermath of lying on the ground at an art gallery.

"Hark! Caesar is turned to hear. What's next?" my dad asked. "Bear wrestling? Volcano diving?"

My mother sighed, but I could hear her smiling. "Just promise you'll call before you do anything that requires a waiver."

"It wasn't a waiver, Mom. I am a provisionally licensed paragliding pilot," I reminded her. "Where can I fly us in the next thirty days before it expires?"

My dad laughed and my mother paused to consider whether I was joking. Truthfully, I would *never do it again*. But wasn't it sort of wonderful to do something so unnecessarily dumb? To work against my own dark determinism? I have worshipped at the altar of productivity for too long. I have successfully outmaneuvered naps, hobbies, and simple pleasures straight into middle age. Watch me take any hour and divide it into a thousand uses!

Some truths exist to keep us alive. Like: *Check the expiration date.* Or: *Find your people.* Or: *Unless you remember going to flight school, you are not a pilot.* But perhaps some things that keep us alive are less obvious, truths that will cause us to take the long way, ruin our schedules, and sweep the ground clear out from under our feet.

40

Ways to (Almost) Guarantee Joy for No Reason

WELCOME TO WHAT my sister Maria calls No Reason Season. Congratulations! You are getting off the superhighways of efficiency! You are saying "No!" to usefulness! Stop sprinting toward self-mastery and have some experiences that are not for any reason *except your delight.*

1. Host a taste-test party. It can be for anything—ketchup, generic colas, best vanilla ice cream, fast-food french fries. Remove the labels and have everyone rank their favorites.

2. Pretend you are in a sitcom the next time you meet a stranger. Life is much funnier if you imagine a laugh track playing in the background.

3. Dress as your favorite nineties album cover. Do it solo. Or invite others in on the fun. (Secondhand clothing stores have everything you need for time travel.)

4. Make up weirdly specific songs about your pet. Or sing seventies love ballads to them, inserting their names: "Hold me closer, Tiny Hazelnut!"

5. Wear your most sparkly outfit to your next appointment or meeting. Declare it is Sequin Friday or Sparkle Tuesday and be surprised other people didn't get the memo.

6. Fold your toilet paper into tiny origami like at a fancy hotel. Bonus points if you can figure out how to make animals out of towels and surprise your roommate with a towel sloth on the counter.

7. Keep premade cookie dough in the freezer for any and all occasions. Sprinkle a little salt on the top because *who can stop you?*

8. Pick a walk-up song for everyone in your home or at the office. Play it as they come in, as LOUDLY AS YOU WANT.

There is more. There is more.

*There is more. There is more. There is more. There is more.
There is more. There is more. There is more. There is more.
There is more. There is more. There is more. There is more.
There is more. There is more. There is more. There is more.
There is more. There is more. There is more. There is more.
There is more. There is more. There is more. There is more.
There is more. There is more. There is more. There is more.
There is more. There is more. There is more. There is more.
There is more. There is more. There is more. There is more.
There is more. There is more. There is more. There is more.
There is more. There is more. There is more. There is more.
There is more. There is more. There is more. There is more.
There is more. There is more. There is more. There is more.
There is more. There is more. There is more. There is more.
There is more. There is more. There is more. There is more.
There is more. There is more. There is more. There is more.
There is more. There is more. There is more. There is more.
There is more. There is more. There is more. There is more.
There is more. There is more. There is more. There is more.
There is more. There is more. There is more. There is more.
There is more. There is more. There is more. There is more.
There is more. There is more. There is more. There is more.
There is more. There is more. There is more. There is more.
There is more. There is more. There is more. There is more.
There is more. There is more. There is more. There is more.
There is more. There is more. There is more. There is more.
There is more. There is more. There is more. There is more.
There is more. There is more. There is more. There is more.
There is more. There is more. There is more. There is more.
There is more. There is more. There is more. There is more.
There is more. There is more. There is more. There is more.*

PART
IV

Living

41

The Biggest Tiny Thing You Can Do

A RETIRED PROFESSOR WITH a terminal cancer diagnosis asks me, a stranger, to have coffee with him early in the morning. I find him in the lobby of a Victorian-era hotel sitting by a grand southern window, the light pouring in over the table, over the coffee in his lightly trembling hands. We will spend the next hour talking through how he should spend the last months of his life. What should he do with the time? How should he close out this great experiment? I don't know. I have never died before. But, like all professors, I like to be a good teacher. And he wants to be a good student. So we take out our scratch paper and our pens and sketch out ways he could live out his own capstone assignment.

Right before I get up to leave he says, "Wait, sorry, I haven't asked you anything about yourself. Are you working on anything of your own?" he says, trying to rally a little energy.

"I'm working on becoming more joyful," I say, taking my linen blazer from the back of my chair.

"And have you figured that out?" he asks, putting on his glasses to see me better.

"I have, a little bit," I say. "Lately I've been better about setting myself up to be surprised by joy." I think about the leaping off cliffs, and the wrestling with sharks.

"I wonder if you might consider making a list," he says.

"I already made one," I report, like a student turning in her homework. Truly, haven't I already done quite enough with The List?

"Make a list of things you *still* want to change," he persists, taking out a fresh piece of paper. "Just try right now for a moment. I won't look."

I really have to get back to the office, but there is something very strange about a conversation without reciprocity. And didn't he used to teach social innovation and moral formation? I feel the pull toward my own calendar crumble, and I sit back down. I slide the paper toward me and start to write out the first few items of the original List. *Restaurant Family. Allowing people to pretend I can handle chronic illness on my own. Doctors who don't believe me.* No, wait, I crossed that last one off after I met the nurse. That was wonderful.

"Okay," his voice cuts right through my thoughts. "Now cross off anything on that list you can't do anything about."

I stare at most of the items. I couldn't exactly *fix* the Restaurant Family situation, but it feels strange to cross off the word *family*, so I leave it. What about just the regular leftovers of resentment and doing things I don't want to do for the rest of time?

"I want you to ask yourself if anything you wrote down is beyond your sphere of influence," he continued mercilessly. I look again at the entries that, by this point, I've mostly memorized. "Anything you can't influence," the professor continues. "Give up! Sorry. Time to move on."

I start crossing off the remaining items. Soon there is almost nothing left on my list.

"What's something you can do *something* about, but not *a lot* about?" he says, tearing open a new packet of sugar for his coffee. "Most people would say that if you can't do *a lot,* do *nothing.* Can you see anything on that list that's small?"

I consider this.

"No, most of these things are pretty big."

"Don't think big! If you want to change, think small, start small," he says. "Small is beautiful."

Small is beautiful, I repeat to myself. I think of a couple I know and adore. Married and in their sixties, they recently lost both their adult sons, one to cancer, and one to the disease of despair. Now when this couple wakes up in the morning, they need to stay in bed for a few hours. They might do their devotionals, watch a television show, or call their therapist. Waking up to a world without your children takes the time it takes. But when they finally get out of bed, this is what they do: they make friends with strangers; they buy gifts for other people's grandchildren; they swim in the ocean. They perform small miracles.

Thinking about them reminds me of something that writer and pastor Jeff Chu likes to pray: *God, grant me appropriate smallness.* In a world that is overwhelming and full of suffering, give me back the smallness that is mine. Small actions. Small attempts. Small miracles.

I pull the paper a little closer to me and write out a few

new options in my neatest print so the professor can't see it. I can barely see it myself.

- Continue to Add to THE LIST when People deserve it because Otherwise I will go BANANAS and Gaslight Myself.
- Check THE LIST Regularly to see IF there are ANY I can CROSS off by Ritualizing the Grief of them.
- PRay for that Lovely Gift of PeACe we GEt sometimes about What NeveR CHanges.
- Keep Shaking UP that overly cautious Fear in my BONES with SoME Reasonable Danger — the TyPE that Makes your MOM Stay by the PHONe
- TALK to PeoPLe about How they found A Little Joy lately

"One last thing," the professor says. "The other mistake people make is trying to do everything on their own. At some point everyone gets stuck. I want you to think back on this breakfast and remind yourself that most things worth doing require some help. I asked you, didn't I?"

I smile. That sounds about right. I lean over to give him a hug goodbye but mostly succeed in getting my hair in his coffee.

"I don't know if I will see you, but I like knowing that we both have work to do," I say, giving his shoulder a squeeze.

"You want to be more joyful," he says again, clearly. "Make a list. Keep it small. Ask for help."

42

Expect a Miracle

I SPENT YEARS STUDYING the pioneers of televangelism and, in particular, a man named Oral Roberts. He was a genius at slogans. *God is a good God!* he would say, which was pithy and hard to argue with. The audience began to want good things from the God who was good.

Oral Roberts had a rich, low voice and, even in a suit, he looked like a lumberjack deciding whether to save time by wrestling the tree from the earth with his bare hands. When the preaching was over, he used to move into the part of the church service devoted to miraculous healing. People with various psychological and physical afflictions would line up in the aisle under his canvas cathedrals (and later the university he named after himself) and approach the edge of the stage where he stood, looming. He would take off his suit jacket, roll his cotton shirt up over his enormous forearms, and place his hands on the head, or shoulders, arms, or legs of the person in line. (Pelvises and anything bordering on genitals always got a very nice, general head pat from him with a verbal description instead.) "Expect a miracle," he would say to the people patiently waiting in line for their turn. Expect a miracle.

A miracle is, by definition, an overriding of the natural order. The laws of cause and effect seem to no longer apply. I know people like to soften the definition by leaps and bounds, by making the miraculous an exercise in perception: e.g., *it's a miracle to me*. I didn't expect, say, the Yale basketball team to win the national championship ever because the odds weren't great and then they do and suddenly it's a miracle. Well, no, it was unexpected. It did not press pause on normal operations of space and time to allow something entirely impossible to slip through the cracks of the universe and become possible. But gravity was not reversed. Death did not become life. A miracle is more than a surprise. It's an overturning of the applecart of reasonable expectation.

So when Oral Roberts said, "Expect a miracle!" in his low, Southern drawl, he said it so many times that you might almost forget the friction, the spiritual heat, he was making. Expect a surprise? No, more than that. Expect a miracle! Expect to undo any normal set of beliefs you have about how the world works and whether up is down and down is up. Maybe tumors disappear because you asked God out loud. Maybe little boys with multiple sclerosis drop their walkers and run across the stage into your arms because you ask them if they have Jesus in their hearts. Maybe people who die don't stay dead because you asked, you pleaded, you begged, and your heart was pure. Expect what you've never seen happen and no one you've ever met has either.

Miracle-thinking asks you to tug on all the threads. What if everything is possible? After all, God is the good kind of God. And I used to imagine that the most faithful sort of person never settled for less than everything.

But I realize now how much wisdom is found when a miracle never comes. When not everything is possible. And how beautiful it is to be deeply hopeful, anyway.

I wanted to ask my friend, theologian Jerry Sittser, about how he has managed the ongoingness of a life that needed a miracle—and never got one. He was in his early forties when he lost his mother, wife, and young daughter when their car was struck head-on by a drunk driver.

That was some thirty years ago, and I called him one gray afternoon to ask him a little more about what sense he has made of his loss ever since.

It was an insurmountable tragedy. He was left alone to parent three young children, one of whom had been seriously injured in the accident, and every moment of the day held some terrible reminder of the love he had lost. He tried to duplicate all their beautiful routines—all their ways of being a family—but those first months and years were excruciating.

"Did anyone say anything useful at all?" I asked, doubtfully. What words can stand when so much has fallen?

Jerry sat back on his couch, and gave the question a moment to breathe. "Well, I did have a good friend tell me that denial was not an option." He chuckled, a bitter sound. "The experience was too big and too catastrophic to avoid. It was a kind of sorrow that penetrated beyond the depths."

I watched the tears form in his eyes, and he rubbed his forehead as if to erase the thought. He waited a long moment before he continued. "I had to figure out how to live for my children, even as I was grieving the three generations of women who were lost in an instant. One love cannot take the place of the other. You have to learn how to do both."

I paused, chewing on my question. "I want to ask you about something that feels hard to say because I know we're both very careful about not trying to rush to solve the problem of pain. But I've heard you say before that loss has a very mysterious way of expanding us and making us more somehow . . ."

He nodded thoughtfully as I circled around the question.

"I don't want to sound like I'm . . . you know . . ."

He raised a hand and waved it away, as if to absolve me from saying the words. "I know what you're asking, and the answer is one of the secrets to life: we need to live in this tension."

I nodded, relieved.

He continued: "I remember thinking: I wish that my wife could see the kind of father I have become because of her death. And the bitter irony is that it's her absence that helped me discover it. What do you do with that? Well, you just live with it."

Looking at a man who had done that—lived with it—for thirty years, I felt such a rush of awe. Here he was in retirement, after having carried every joy and sorrow with him.

I smiled back at him, ignoring the tears forming in my own eyes. "There is so much beauty and, in the grand scheme of things, such an unbearable amount of pain," I said. "I have started thinking of it like an aperture, you know, just the widening to be able to take in all the light . . . and the darkness."

"Oh, that's a good term," he said with a smile. "Suffering is like a blinding light and all of a sudden the aperture closes. And then it opens and closes and opens and closes many times every day. Somehow, we have to become attuned to both. I love the story of Lazarus for that exact reason. Jesus raises him from the dead. We are all longing for resurrection—but we forget that there will be another death. I mean, Lazarus did die again. And that is the dirty little secret about miracles . . . they don't last."

I laughed, but it came out as a sort of startled sound. Expect a miracle? He was right. Every lovely thing must be accepted for what it is—temporary.

"It feels like you're kind of stabbing me when you say that, Jerry. Even good things don't last."

"And there's nothing wrong with that," he said. "It's only human to long for those reversals or solutions of one kind or another. But it's a little random. We take our chances that all things considered, life is worth living," he concluded, and it felt, for a moment, like he had poured his whole life's wisdom into my unsteady hands.

43

God Bless Us Everyone

It was a sold-out performance, which pleased me to no end. I had had to buy the tickets months in advance to secure my seat in the historic theater, which sat in the heart of a small North Carolina town at least an hour away. This newly refurbished triumph of lacquer and red velvet gave home to a community's hopes and the annual performance of the timeless classic *A Christmas Carol*.

I normally like to picture the baby Jesus as the celebrity of December, but this year it was Henry, my now-retired psychologist. A true behaviorist, he exemplifies a belief in the power of the type of right-sized, concrete actions my professor friend had probably been talking about when he advised me to "keep it small." And since retiring, Henry had worked his way up from monologues to regular local theater productions, and now, here he was: center stage.

When the curtains parted, Scrooge the former psychologist walked onstage, utterly transformed. The man with a gentle face and an attentive expression looked positively stooped by a lifetime of resentments and solitary bitterness. He played the miserly, embittered Scrooge like he had never known a day of gladness. He was, true to the character, a complete dick to all who loved him. He raged against his nephew's hospitality, the poor's neediness, and the uselessness of parties. By the time he was confronted by the ghosts, he had harrumphed his way through his heartless past, his refusal of present joys, and his desolate future. We watched how he hated the world that did not love him back.

But I could not get over the crying. Henry's Scrooge cried. He began when he realized that he had misused his life and squandered every good gift, but was he supposed to cry during the *entire* second act?

Then, the ghosts fell away, the bell struck midnight, and Scrooge was back in his nightgown in his own room, returned to the living just in the nick of time: he can change.

And he is filled with joy.

"I don't know what to do!" Scrooge says, laughing, returned by the ghosts and dumped off in the familiarity of his bedroom. He is euphoric. "I am as light as a feather, I am as happy as an angel, I am as merry as a school-boy. I am as giddy as a drunken man!"

But tell that to his face.

Scrooge cried and cried until long, thundering applause insisted that he take a deep bow, and when the curtains fell, I clapped and whistled until my palms were red and ears were ringing.

I waited by the stage door as the crowds thinned and Bob Cratchit found his wife and Tiny Tim was collected by his parents. Scrooge emerged with watery eyes still streaking eyeliner down his chalky cheeks. I couldn't help but reach for a hug when I saw him.

I asked, immediately: "Are you okay?"

He chuckled softly. "I'm okay."

"What brought up so much emotion? You're an amazing actor and maybe you felt *nothing,* but there is also a lot going on with the character."

"It's just . . ." He paused. "Scrooge is so grateful. And I am so, so *grateful.*"

I wanted to ask him why. Was Henry grateful to have been able to use his gifts so masterfully? Was it because it is just so lovely to be part of something bigger than yourself? Was there something private he wouldn't want to tell me about his deep relief that he had been given back the world as it is?

There is a crystalline quality to the way I think back on that night, about Scrooge, remembering him shuffling around, grateful and tired and very, very weepy. About how he had been taken through the past and present and future, and was horrified by what he saw: selfishness, greed, stubbornness, indifference, a life atrophied from lack of love. And about how Scrooge laughed and laughed as though he were entirely out of practice. He had heard the bell strike midnight and felt so very very lucky, and seemed to know a little more about how joy thaws our hearts and quickens us.

For a moment, our heartbreak does not matter. It does not matter. It does not matter.

We are alive—like Lazarus, briefly resurrected. Whatever has weighed down our souls is gone and our spirits lift *up, up, up.*

Joy is, at bottom, the belief that existence is good. That *to be* is good.

This is why it coexists with suffering, why it *cannot be separated* from suffering. Because suffering is what raises the question, what draws each of us into the howling pain of a single individual—alone, lost, misunderstood—and then raises the challenge: Is it still good to be? Is it still worth it? Is it a blessing, and not a prison sentence?

Because often, as faithful existentialist philosopher Kierkegaard reminds us, "Life is a dark saying."

There is nothing negative or ungrateful about recognizing this—everyone, at all times and places, if they are honest, knows it. Life is so beautiful and life is so hard. We wish we were doing mountaintop yoga but instead we are managing the ache and complaining over the phone.

But then joy, when it comes, is unexpected. It replies not with reasoned argument or detailed logic, but with experience, with perception, with feeling, with *being*.

Joy can come in when you least expect it. But it is more than just a feeling, it is an argument for life itself. Joy is the idea that, yes, it is good to exist—*even now*. Even in the midst of horrible suffering. It is the ultimate yes.

"Suppose that we said yes to a single moment," wrote Friedrich Nietzsche, "then we have not only said yes to ourselves, but to the whole of existence." We have all had moments when we felt this way, when we knew that everything mattered, that everything was how it should be. We look into our child's eyes. We see a rainbow. We say *yes* to our place among the trees.

But Nietzsche wants to carry this forward—even into sorrow.

Have you ever said Yes to one joy?
Oh my friends, then you also said Yes to all pain.
All things enchained, entwined, enamored—
if you ever wanted one time two times,
if you ever said "I like you, happiness!
Whoosh! Moment!" then you wanted everything back!

This yes, this affirmation—it encompasses all times and places. Saying yes to one joy is saying yes to all pain, because it all comes together. Nietzsche continues: "For nothing stands alone, either in ourselves or in things; and if our soul did but once vibrate and resound with a chord of happiness, then all of eternity was necessary to bring forth this one occurrence—and in this single moment when we said yes, all of eternity was embraced, redeemed, justified and affirmed."

It is good to be. That is why our suffering is so intolerable—that is why it is so mystifying to us. We know that when we are stuck in the basement, when we feel lead in our souls, that there is something deeply wrong about a world that stops making sense. Suffering makes us question everything. But so does joy.

"It's a gift to exist," said comedian Stephen Colbert in an interview about the death of his father and brothers. "It's a gift to exist."

It's a gift to exist! cried Scrooge, my friend.

Even now. Today.

There is a really funny description from the very serious C. S. Lewis about how you know you are experiencing joy: it stabs you, Lewis said. Joy is a *stab of longing*.

No wonder Henry didn't stop crying. We could not be more grateful, more delighted, more hopeful about the world being given back to us for a moment. We might have just been stabbed, but that's how we know that we are joyful, anyway.

44

Surprising Moments Other People Have Found Joy: A List

1. "I was so mad at my mom. Years and years of being angry. One day she was outside in the yard planting flowers, and while she bent over to pick up some petunias she must have tweaked her back because she suddenly seized up like it was a heart attack. I knew she was fine, but she was so dramatic about the way she fell forward onto the rest of the flowers that I ran outside to her and, while she was lying on the ground, she looked at me expecting me to be worried, but I was crying—crying with laughter. I mean, I *wept*. Then we both started laughing. I swear that opened up some surreal forgiveness between us."

2. "We had been trying to have kids for such a long time and it wasn't in the cards. We were pursuing adoption and we found out that there was a mother nearby considering us. We interviewed and when that phone call came saying 'Come pick up your baby boy!' it was the single greatest moment of my life."

3. "I had just ended my engagement and could not get over how much I had disappointed everyone in my life: my ex-fiancé, his family, our friends, even my family. I was helping my friend, who works at a church, close up for the night and she cranked up some music over the speaker system. The hymn 'It Is Well with My Soul' started playing and I lay back on the pew and let myself sob, but even as I cried, I felt good for the first time in a long time. I think that's joy: *it is well with my soul*."

4. "My son has this incredible belly laugh with the rasp and pitch of someone who is eighty years old. He throws his head back and unleashes it for the whole world to enjoy. I've found healing in his joyful bellows."

5. "My marriage was falling apart. I took a trip to visit a friend to clear my head, and I was walking around his farm field with a bunch of his goats. I know it sounds weird, but one of the goats was so calming and when I looked into his eyes I remembered how long it had been since I felt seen by God. And, then, suddenly, this huge feeling of love came rushing back. Then I was so weirdly happy. I think that's joy. I couldn't stop crying, and I'm *not* a guy who cries . . . and I really hope I don't have to become a vegetarian."

6. "As part of my work with International Justice Mission, I was traveling with a remarkable young woman who is a survivor of online sexual exploitation. She had chosen the pseudonym 'Joy' to keep her real identity safe. To this day, I think of joy as a young woman cooking her favorite Fili-

pino dish, giggling in that kitchen as we all helped pour and smooth ingredients together. Sometimes these simple joys are the hardest to notice because they are so typical, but it's important to pin down these moments and treasure them—not feeling guilty for being able to have them or rushing to the next 'important' agenda item. Joy is everywhere."

45

The Task

THE CEMETERY WAS spread like a picnic in the center of the forest, an unexpected blanket of green grass with a tangle of trees closed in a conspiracy around the dead. Whoever had been tasked with the solemn duty of laying out each plot had likely been the same mind who carved the sharply bending road around every outcropping of sugar maples and black gums with a scalpel, as if each were sacred, as if not one could be spared to the axe.

Every spring tree in these soft foothills of Pennsylvania was ready to burst with possibility and so, it seemed, was every college graduate I'd seen earlier that day as they received their diplomas at a nearby university. I had been asked to give a commencement address—one part inspiration and one part commission. Delivering commencement addresses always leaves me feeling like I'm giving an unwanted eulogy to someone else's family. Gone is your innocence! Ahead is the burden of responsibility! And yet, the pageantry of youth goes on, uninterrupted. A strong minority of young men will always wait to use the single moment they are onstage in front of their parents to yell something perfectly incoherent while pumping their hands above their heads; and a majority of the young women will have inexplicably decided to brave stilettos, even though the choice will require heavy use of the handrail to get up the steps and will leave them teetering like baby fawns (warning: first-time walkers!). Onstage next to them, I remember, oh, this is still barely beyond labor and delivery.

That morning, the adults filled the stadium with their nerves, staring at the distant outlines of their children with such concentrated power that, if properly harnessed, could end American reliance on foreign oil. Sorry, Saudi Arabia! Gentle parenting is here. *Are you hungry? Do you have enough boxes to pack up your dorm room? I edited your résumé, but you're going to have to send it out.* They sat there, clutching their programs, with that pang of parental alarm that rings a thousand times a day. But watching their children process, they began to understand that society will no longer praise them for their forceful worry. Come graduation, parents are officially out of a job.

After I'd delivered my speech, taken the requisite photos, and turned in my university-issued gown, I made my way to Charlie's car and hopped into the passenger's seat. Charlie has been hired by the university to chauffeur me around for the day. He had fetched me from my hotel that morning and waited during the ceremonies. Now, after forty minutes of riding in companionable quiet, I looked at the map on my phone again and glanced over at Charlie bent over the wheel of the black sedan, his creased face almost pressed against the windshield as he craned his neck to see around every hairpin turn. We had known each other for only a few hours, and I was already putting our relationship to the test.

Tragically, the World's Largest Bobblehead was too far away and the Peeps factory that pumps out 5.5 million yellow nightmares a day did not offer public tours. I would have to sit at my departure gate for hours or learn more about a historically notable woman named Mary. I chose Mary. But now, poor Charlie. As the road narrowed further, instead of complaining he simply let out a little grunt on every turn as his hands vigorously worked the wheel.

"Well, I don't think we can go much further," he said at last, pulling the car over to the narrow ditch beside the road. "We'll have to walk from here, but it's just there." He jabbed his finger toward the front windshield. Then he swung open his door and moved around to mine with surprising agility.

Under direct sunlight, Charlie looked positively translucent. The word *retired* conjures up images of silver hair and dinners with tablecloths, but Charlie had passed through that portal into what the poet Christian Wiman calls a "wild old age." As I watched him set out along the gravel road by foot, carefully taking each step, I grimaced.

"I'm sorry this has become such a chore. We don't have to do this," I protested. I couldn't make out his face, only his profile.

"Oh," he replied with a little shake of the head, "I don't have anything better to do."

There were still clouds of yellow dust where the heavy tires had chewed through the rocks, but how quickly we watched the trees absorb it, leaving the air crisp and cool.

After a time, we came upon the first line of graves, which were pleasingly laid out like a row of cards placed face down. The names were easy enough to read, chiseled neatly into stone, some flat against the earth and others standing or leaning upright.

"So, who are you looking for again?" he asked.

"Oh, shoot," I said, looking left and right. Grave after grave went on by the hundreds across the pasture. "I didn't think about how to . . ."

"Don't worry," he clucked. "We'll find your people."

Your people. I pressed my lips together involuntarily. Right. That would have made a lot more sense.

We walked the first few rows together at a contemplative pace, mentioning anything that was unusually old or poignant about love that goes on and on.

"Who are *your* people?" I asked, my eyes on the tombstones.

"Oh, I've had lots of people. So many people I might hardly remember their names if I didn't love them so much."

He had grown up in a large family, he explained, with eight boys, three girls. So there was always trouble and noise and hardly a scrap of food in sight except for what he earned and received in kind at a German sausage-making factory. "All of us kids were earning sausages by fourteen and were lucky for it," he assured me. I could see he was starting to settle into a story, and I felt my shoulders drop a little. I wasn't so much buying time as it was being handed to me, and I'd take it.

"Sausages are a commitment," I observed, clearing one row and beginning another. "I had a teacher in high school who worked at a sausage factory on the weekend, and he tried to restrict his meat handling to only one hand. That way on the way home he could crack the window and let his arm hang out the bus because he reeked of red meat."

The old man observed me for a moment and then nodded like we were getting somewhere.

"A job will do that to you."

I finished an inventory of the next row by the time Charlie finished recounting his early adult years selling knives. We had found our own rhythm, him two-stepping around each grave and me checking the names against one on my phone with a regular murmur of interest. But there was a pause after I understood that he and his wife could not have children of their own, and I realized that he had stopped walking. I turned around and saw that his eyes were wet.

"But wouldn't you know? We heard there were boys in our own town, boys in trouble. So my wife and I signed right up. The judge would sentence them to a facility or they could choose to live with us and wouldn't you know? By the time the boys came around, I felt prepared. You have to be a little delinquent to survive ten brothers and sisters." He pressed his sleeves into his eyes and cleared his throat unselfconsciously, giving me a moment to let his words pass through me, circle back, and land.

I met a writer a few years ago named Sarah Sentilles, who had also been a foster parent. She had taken children into her home in exchange for a stipend and her entire soul. The state had categorized this kind of love, that between adults and children not their own, as *stranger care*. Only family can love family, it seemed to imply. There are bonds of commitment and affection only made in blood. But Sarah had carved other people's initials into the soft timber of her flesh and there they stayed: she loved the baby in her arms, loved the undergrown biological mother who would eventually want her baby returned, and loved more children come and gone.

"What did you say the name was?" asked Charlie, sharply returning me to the present.

I paused and looked down again at my phone.

"Mary Reeser," I read off the screen.

"All right," said Charlie, scanning the horizon. "I think we're going to need to have a little chat with the gravedigger."

•   •   •

The gravedigger and maintenance man were one and the same, and we found him under the awning of an enormous shed servicing a faulty riding mower. When he heard us approach, he pulled himself out from under the John Deere hood and thrust his hand out to shake ours.

"Who can I help you with?" he asked, pulling off his baseball cap.

"Is that a zero-turn mower?" I asked instead.

"Yes, ma'am, it is."

"And you can make most of the adjustments you need to cut the grass around the graves?"

"Well, it does fine work with the larger spaces but then I need to return with the Weedwacker to get the job done right," he said undeterred.

"Dammit," I said loudly, which startled them both. "Sorry, I just . . . sorry. I lost an argument."

The men chose that moment of silence not to unsettle me further.

"Look," I said, though no one was looking for anything, "when I was dying of cancer I wanted to buy a plot near my husband's family farm. It was an extremely affordable $250. But then one day my father-in-law asks if I want to buy *his* grave in the plot because he and my mother-in-law have decided to be cremated and—*phumpt*—dumped together in one grave. To save money? Probably. But then I said I didn't want to be smooshed right up beside them: I would buy that plot and my own and use the middle plot to plant a tree."

"Oh, I see," said the gravedigger, who probably did see.

"But they said, 'Absolutely not. We're not mowing around a tree.' And I said that a zero-turn mower would do the trick."

The man squinted and placed his hand on the mower as if grounding himself in the reality of what was happening, but I pressed on. "So I figured I would buy the two graves I wanted, come in at night and plant a tree. It would have to be a tree that's really fast-growing. I'm hoping that by the time anyone notices it, it's going to be too large and cost-prohibitive to cut down." I did not add that Mennonites are so notoriously cheap that it was incredibly savvy of me to use the cost of a sapling against them—cheap vs. cheap—but I planned on telling them next.

Charlie took a moment to digest this exchange. Then turned back to the man. "We're looking for Mary Reeser."

• • •

The stone was much simpler than I expected:

MARY H. REESER

1884–1951

I glanced over at Charlie, who stood a few steps back to give me a quiet moment.

"Not my people," I said, at last. "I'm sorry I didn't say it earlier."

"I did start to get the idea eventually."

"I imagine it was sometime around . . ."

"When the gravedigger mentioned that this woman somehow *exploded*?" he finished.

I laughed and shifted uncomfortably. I didn't want to argue that I had spared him from driving three hours to see a five-foot tombstone for a horse named Mack and a town named Panic.

"Go ahead then," he urged. "Tell me the story."

I pulled out my phone and, increasingly pink from embarrassment, began to read.

"Mary Reeser was a widow in her sixties. The last thing anyone knows for sure is that she had settled in for the evening in her overstuffed chair, that she took two sleeping pills and she was smoking a cigarette. Apparently she caught fire and died."

"Well that's very sad," said Charlie.

"It is," I said.

And we fell silent for a time, quieted by the warmth of whatever sun broke through the dappled leaves.

Charlie squinted at the sky and looked back at me, barely able to feign disinterest. "But what's this about exploding?"

"Well," I said hurriedly, already a little too quick to feel like I could move on. "By the time firefighters arrived on the scene, all that was left was a heavy pile of ashes along with most of her left foot. And the foot *was still wearing the slipper*."

We both leaned over the grave this time. "So this is only her leg," I said, relieved that Charlie was interested instead of deeply annoyed. Now I was ready for a fully theatrical finish. "And the whole thing was so mysterious that the newspapers called her the 'cinder lady' and it was reported to the FBI and investigated as perhaps the best known case of *spontaneous human combustion.*"

"Oooooooh," he said and shivered. "And you brought me here."

"I did," I said, still not entirely sure why.

We both stood up and regarded each another, closer now that we had been connected in this way.

"How did you know?!" he said. The awe in his voice was unmistakable.

"Wait, know what?"

"Well," he said, beginning the long walk to the car, and I fell in beside him. "One time I was sitting at the kitchen table with my wife. Married sixty-four years, you know. And we were talking about something upsetting, I can't remember what, but I started to feel warm. *Very* warm." He put his hand on his chest. "And I began to think, OH NO, HERE WE GO!"

"This is how you go up in flames?" I replied, hardly able to keep my face arranged into concern.

"But then I calmed down." He chuckled, then, sobered, gave me an even look. "But I was warned."

He told me that on long nights driving for the limo service he liked to listen to a radio call-in show and had been in rapt attention when the subject turned to spontaneous combustion. In fact, he was quite the expert on the subject.

"Did you know that there are at least forty-nine cases

where someone just goes *poof*? And they're gone? A firefighter called into the show. The victim had burned a hole straight through the floor and the firefighter had to scoop a heap of soot and some of the bigger bones off the basement floor."

I shook my head.

"But you didn't know that I was almost a victim?" he said. He shuddered. "Well. Well. That's really something."

The sun was beating down on us by the time we got back into the sedan, and we waited a few moments for the air-conditioning to catch up before it felt like the right moment to come back to his revelation.

"That was very kind of you to go on that adventure with me," I said. "That was a lot of walking and . . . I hope this isn't rude, but do you mind telling me how old you are?"

"Eighty-four," he announced, a touch of pride in his voice. We were turning back onto the highway now.

"Wow," I said, suddenly remembering his trembling hands lifting my suitcases and how his suit jacket billowed around him. I couldn't tell from the stories he was telling me if he *had* to work or if he *wanted* to work, and I wondered if having to work at his age felt more like a tragedy.

"What is the best advice for being eighty-four?" I asked.

He looked chuffed, which pleased me. "My wife and I always said that we felt like we were supposed to be doing something special with our lives—that we were *called* to something—but then fifteen years went by." He made a little *phfff* sound. "Nothing. Nothing happened at all."

"Oh no," I said, remembering that feeling of the ache. The dark determinism. The longing and the silence in return.

"I was really unhappy, and I could tell that I was headed in a bad way. So I decided to see this as a day-by-day thing. And I really mean that. It's day by day."

"What does that look like?" I asked, leaning forward to make sure I caught every word over the sound of the engine.

"If you love the people God puts in your way, well... you'll always be busy. You take it day by day. So every day, I'm not just taking things as they come. I am tasked. You see the difference? This isn't random. I'm *tasked* with love."

I thought about all the people who Charlie had loved, and all the foster children he had made into family. I remembered his wife of six decades and the hilarious acceptance with which he loved listening to the stories of strangers, however explosive.

We meet people every day who manage obligations without love. Serve without love. Hands that feed without a heart that beats.

Charlie's philosophy was elegant in its simplicity: Love the people in your way, every day. Accept love as an assignment.

"And that love gave you a sense of purpose?" I asked.

I once read a lovely moral triptych attributed to eighteenth-century philosopher Immanuel Kant about how to be truly joyful.

1. Find something to do.

2. Find someone to love.

3. Find something to hope for.

It seemed to me that Charlie knew how to be propelled into joy by the daily work of love. As the great theologian Karl Barth argued, joy is a gift and a task. Joy gives you a job.

"Oh yes," he said. "Otherwise it's too easy to get distracted. When you're this age, you genuinely do not know what you'll be able to do in a month or a year. But today? Well, today was you!"

I grinned. I could have hugged him right then, but I waited until he pulled up to the curb of the airport terminal. I got out and, still horrified, allowed him to pull my luggage from the trunk when he wouldn't have it any other way. I embraced him then, his small frame squeezing me just as tightly.

"Thank you for giving me the assignment. It's been so good to conquer today with you," I said, turning toward the airport. But then I remembered something.

"Charlie? About the whole spontaneous combustion thing. I want you to know, on a pastoral note, if you ever feel it start up again, I believe you will survive."

"Oh, thank you, dear," he said, looking much more relaxed after I said it. "It's a hard way to go."

(LiviNg = the AChe + Joy)

46

Ways I Have Been Tasked with Love Lately: An Incomplete List

1. The school drop-off in the morning is a consistently failed experiment in sandwich assembly and time management, but, if I make it with five minutes to spare, my son lets me hold his hand for half a block before people can see us.

2. The Best Friend and I have an "immersive therapy weekend" on the books, where we are going to a location that promises foraging, boat building, and cod fishing. I have promised her that I will be the one who baits the hooks with leeches, if she starts from the beginning and tells me *everything* about her new job promotion and anything that has made The List lately.

3. Started volunteering at a housing facility for out-of-towners getting cancer treatment, which gives women a break from caregiving. I am now an expert in making spaghetti while old men explain what radiation has done to their prostates.

4. Choosing not to roll my eyes about my husband's Pickleball Playoff Season after I realized how much he laughs when he plays.

5. Letting the ache feel more like a reminder that today I want more, more of everything, forever. Amen.

47

Ka-boom

LATE SPRING WAS turning into a very showy summer, and I couldn't wait to get my family into cheap bathing suits and yell at them about sunscreen. I had agreed to do a series of summer lectures in upstate New York because it was a short enough distance away for Toban to drive us there in the truck towing an Airstream while Zach waited in the back seat clutching his metal detector, eager to be released into a world of unsuspecting aluminum cans.

We would be spending the week at the Chautauqua Institution, which warmed my historical heart. It had been founded in the nineteenth century by Methodist preachers who created a kind of outdoor symposium where speakers, musicians, pastors, politicians, and business leaders could speak to crowds interested in progressive social causes and spiritual improvement. Four hours into the drive and I was playing my part on schedule—having put on about eight pounds from hot dogs and the kind of camping-related stress that comes from a woman pretending in a Ford F-150 that she does not, in fact, need access to high-speed wireless and double monitors.

It always seems to go like this. I plan the trips—every meticulous detail—as part of a grand strategy to make everyone happy. Pickleball paddles are packed! Treasure maps are in process! But then there is not one single moment of the day in which I don't wonder if I should be solving a personal problem, compensating for someone's discomfort, or answering an email. Plus, I should really start working on one of the lectures I am going to deliver. I always think I'm going to be a different person on vacation, but then I also remember that this is *not a vacation, it is a family trip.*

As fifteenth-century mystic Thomas à Kempis observed: "You cannot escape it, run where you will; for wherever you go, you take yourself with you."

Yes. Wherever I go, there I am. But within twenty-four hours I was settled into the Chautauqua Institution's splendid showcase of opera and sprawling orchestras and a daily round-robin of speakers and worship services in their enormous outdoor amphitheater. If I must be with myself somewhere, this was a good enough place to be.

I stood at the lectern and stared out at the crowd: "How many people are sixty years old? Seventy years old? Wait, over eighty years old?" I tried to make each decade wave their hands like they just don't care until that really started slowing us down. Well, that accounted for almost everyone. Except the dogs. Maybe a hundred dogs also attended my lecture on our culture's over-insistence on happiness. At the end I received the slowest standing ovation I have ever received in my life.

One of the salient facts you learn when you give public

speeches on a regular basis is that some people—and by *some* people I mean *old* people—will brook no nonsense. They will tolerate zero guff. And they know precisely how the wheat ought to be separated from the chaff, and they tell you to your face in the meet-and-greet time afterward. I respect that a great deal because I, too, when faced with a limited horizon, began doing and saying things that surprised even me. (I recently ran into one of the custodians from my university and she was with a friend, and she introduced me by saying matter-of-factly: "This is that sick professor who hates bullshit that I was telling you about." I laughed too loudly at that, then sometime later in the day I realized I was also surprisingly moved.)

After my lecture, at the meet and greet, I noticed a gentleman waiting very patiently to say hello. His name was Joe, and all the hair on his head had retreated to his upper lip, his shaggy mustache flapping over a huge smile as he talked.

"I have a problem with your lecture. You see, I'm happy all the time. I don't need that positive-thinking stuff because I'm already happy!"

"Oh, that's great!" I said.

"I'm *really* always happy. Other people might find that a bit hard to take." He glanced at his wife, who I had not noticed a half step behind him, looking very dour. She grimaced.

"WASN'T SHE GREAT THOUGH?" he said, careful to raise his voice so his wife could hear him.

"WHO?"

"HER! THIS LADY RIGHT HERE."

The woman shrugged. "Who can remember all these speakers?"

"Well, I thought you were great," he said, turning to me again with a wink.

His wife, in the meantime, had walked over to the buffet where she stood adrift in a sea of appetizers looking like nothing could tempt her.

"I think it's wonderful that you feel so good," I said, returning my gaze to the mustached man. "Do you think it's your personality? This is your natural state?"

"Oh, well, I think so. I've always been this way."

"That must be a very nice way to be," I mused. "You have a low set point for happiness."

"I do! I'm pretty much always happy. But sometimes . . ." He paused, giving it a bit more thought. "I find it strange. I don't understand why other people feel down. I look at them—people who are depressed—and I think, *What do you have to be upset about?* and it feels like . . ." He pressed his palms out in front of him like he was pushing against a wall.

"There's a barrier between you."

"Yes," he said finally and smiled. He looked over at his wife with her back turned. He seemed to feel like he had strayed too far, and as if by an invisible string, he was being pulled back to her.

I watched him float away, back to his wife—now directing her annoyance at the flutter of the napkins on the table—and he called back: "You keep up the good work!"

But I was plunged into the deep end of what the man had said. I thought of all the people I had met who never felt burdened by deep grief or deep depression or deep much-of-anything. I remembered Todd describing doing chest compressions on a dead man and subsequently conducting a successful job interview. I recalled the puma's promise that an algorithm could optimize for our happiness and minimize our pain if only we would follow the rules.

"What is my life for?" my father has been asking lately.

He has been tripping over failures again. He is seventy-six and he still falls into the same existential tar pit every few months. He tries to rally, to remind himself who he is. "I have been a great teacher. I have launched my girls into the world. I have been a good man." But every few months he is back in the basement with the lights off.

What is my life for?

And then, eventually, his aperture will open and he will pick up the phone when I call as I drive home from work.

"Dad, did I wake you?" I say, knowing full well that I did. There is something that must happen between us, as adults, as two shares of the same soul. Every now and then, it does: I will tell him that he is brave for getting up again today after depression has tried to lawyer him back to bed, and he will drink his breakfast Diet Mountain Dew and sometime before lunch he has already laughed. And somewhere in the nudging and the calling me back later, he will tell me that he is so terribly proud of the person I have become, and that he wishes that I did not feel quite so responsible for everyone anymore. I am willing him into courage, and he is willing me into freedom. On the best of days, everything happened, and there has been some apology.

There is joy in everything.

There is joy in everything except despair.

Novelist Kaveh Akbar has found that deep place: "I hope that when there is laughter, it's laughter made wise by having known real grief—and when there is grief, it is made wise by having known real joy."

Joy brings fireworks that light us up from within. And in a moment of pure aliveness, nothing incomplete matters.

It's not that anything is complete. It's that nothing incomplete matters.

I wouldn't want to take away any of the mustached man's unflappable happiness because, after all, happiness has its place. Happiness, generally speaking, describes a positive disposition about your life's purpose and your everyday circumstances. Happiness means *you're good*. There is nothing frivolous about taking meaningful steps toward becoming a happier person, and it's easy to see that happiness is a cousin to joy. But it's not *joy*.

Joy goes all the way down.

You can't be happy and sad at the same time. But you can be joyful and sad, which is a great trick. Joy is the great mixed-state emotion, meaning that all at once you can feel joy and sorrow and fear and pain—and basically everything else, unfortunately. And fortunately.

Joy is one of the greatest promises of all. It is not a ladder to climb out of any unwanted feeling. In fact, joy takes for granted that you might be miserable some days and that a general "disposition of happiness" is entirely out of reach. We can't always be happy. But still, joy will arrive. We can know in our hearts—we can believe—that joy is a gift meant for us, too.

Joy does not need to wait until you are healed. Joy does not need to take a beat until you have a plan to replace the life you may have lost. It will not even need to be postponed until after your scheduled colonoscopy.

But there are times we must pull joy into our own bodies like drawing a breath.

I asked my friends the other day, the beautiful couple who lost both their adult sons, about whether they allow themselves the gift of joy. They would have every reason not to.

"If I survived all this only to deny myself all these small joys"—he shook his head—"I would be missing out on everything that's left for me."

Yes, joy, give me everything that is left for me.

          •   •   •

The reception was going on and on, and because everyone had a lot of opinions to share with me in the receiving line, it was starting to get a little hot. But another man had been waiting especially patiently and by the time he reached me he launched into his speech at full speed to make up for lost time.

"You are asking us to be more honest with one another about what is difficult instead of pretending to be happy, and I do that. I do. It's called Alcoholics Anonymous. It is an organization begun by . . ." The man, having never introduced himself, was now deep into the history of the recovery moment and his own difficult journey with alcohol. I know a testimony when I hear one. The moment of crisis. The moment of decision. The discovery of something greater capable of saving you, even as you take steps to save yourself. I have heard hundreds of stories like this, stories that describe a miracle. Someone plucked like an ember out of the fire.

The man returned to his point. "We don't know why it works! Why does it work when you sit around with other people like you and speak honestly with one another?" He paused and looked at me intently, just to make doubly sure I was listening. "KA-BOOM," he said, making an exploding sound and miming with his hand, his fingers like a bomb, detonating. "I can't even believe it."

He continued. "You get up in the morning and you don't think you can do it. All you want is a drink. And then you go and sit with some people in a church basement and then what? KA-BOOM." He made another exploding sound.

I started to think about the reasons why this process worked, about accountability and community, about confession and repentance and believing in a God who wants your wholeness . . .

But then the man made his point again. And this time I heard it.

"You get up in the morning, and you're the same person who is probably going to make the wrong decision. And you're suffering and that's life."

He took a deep breath, coming in for a landing. "Life is a spectrum. On one side of the spectrum is pain and suffering. But, on the other side, it isn't happiness . . . It's *mystery*."

I must have looked surprised because he started again. "So it's a regular day and you have no idea how you're going to get through your life. And then you go sit somewhere in a basement with other people and you try. And then something—SOMETHING! WHAT IS IT?—happens." He made another exploding sound.

"You feel better. And you get better. You try. But it doesn't stop there. *Something always happens.* I don't know how else to explain it. Something carries you forward. That is the mystery of every day."

Joy is a mystery: its arrival, its timing, its power, its ability to shout down despair. I believe that joy never abandons us. Isn't that exactly what I had promised my old roommate, that beautiful bride, terrified that she would never know anything but sadness after her mom died? I had promised her this mystery—that we are given back to ourselves again. Yes. I *believe.*

"KA-BOOM!" I said.

"Exactly," he said.

48

The Song

"Too many people die with the song still in them."

A friend handed me those words when I was diagnosed with cancer and, for all the advice I received, this is the piece that has outlasted all the rest. *You are a song—sing it.*

We must take that risk. We must sing the song that's always in us.

I could have sworn that I heard it the other day when the Best Friend answered a call in front of me.

"OH, HEY! Can I . . . um . . . call you back when I'm alone?" Her voice was up at least an octave, and she had turned away from me to do a lot of murmuring before she put her phone back in her purse. I pressed my lips together into what I hoped looked like deferential interest. *Who me? I don't need to find his home address using Google Earth and possibly drive past his workplace to verify his résumé.*

"Will I hate him?" I asked immediately.

She barked a laugh. "Absolutely. Oh, you're going to hate this one."

"Is he married? Does he have a job? Is he funny?"

"No . . . Yes . . . And, he's funny, but I'm definitely funnier. But we're not exactly talking a lot . . ." My eyebrows shot up and she looked over quickly and laughed again. "No, not like that. I met him at that drop-in dance class. He's *meh*. I mean, he's cute enough, but it's not like he's . . ." She closed her eyes and pretended to fan herself.

We sighed dramatically, as if we were old and world-weary, as if we were Rose reflecting back on torrid moments before the *Titanic* sank.

"I like that you're back out there," I said, "and I love that you're doing an activity that genuinely makes you happy. And who knows? This guy could be magical." She glanced away for a microsecond, but I caught it. "But he's *not* magical . . . and you already know it."

"He's a great dancer! He is! He smells good and you *know* I like a man in polo shirts and it feels so good to be moving again. But . . . I looked down the other day and I could have sworn he was wearing *bowling shoes*. Which is fine? But I'm fairly certain they are from that bowling place we went to for my mom's birthday. The shoe size was on the heel!"

"So he bought used bowling shoes . . . or borrowed them . . . or stole them?" I said slowly, because I was on the case.

"Yes! But it's worse than that! He didn't bring socks to class the other day and then I watched him hunt around until he found two plastic bags, which he *wore as socks*."

I paused, giving that revelation a little moment to breathe, but I could feel a light hysteria rising in my chest.

She continued. "Is he going to return the bowling shoes at some point? That's why he can't just let his feet touch the insides of the shoes?"

At this point I was wiping away the first sign of my tears. "Hon, the fact that you were *still* excited when he called . . ."

"I was!" she admitted. "I am! It's so ridiculous."

We were beside ourselves, choking on laughter.

"This is just like the time your date wore tear-away pants to a wine tasting!" I accused, more than happy to load up years and years of unused ammunition.

"He was very tall! It's hard to find pants for very tall people!" she shot back. "I'm not the one who is constantly being talked into algorithm cults at dinners and paying crazy amounts of money for water and breathing advice."

"At least I have never been crapped on by a bird on a date!"

"THAT WAS YOUR WEDDING, KATE!" she shrieked, and we could barely speak because there are so many gloriously ruined wedding photos with her in the background desperately trying to rinse her bridesmaid dress in a decorative fountain. "Well, YOU'RE THE ONE who asks strangers into your car so you can take them deep into the woods!"

Anyone overhearing us would have assumed that each of us was regularly humiliated, catfished, or almost murdered.

So this is not a love story, I thought, looking at her. But I could see there was a fresh light in her eyes. *Maybe not a love story,* I thought. But something. A story about her . . .

Like this.

Licking up more than the crumbs.

Putting meat on those bones.

Feeling the human heart pouring over into something or someone new.

I know that there are times when she feels the ache come roaring back. Her "old friend" sent her a text on her birthday and made sure to let her know when she replied that he is happier than he has ever been. *Fantastic. Elated for him.* But that's the thing about the song that is inside of us: its presence means that all of us non-pumas will never feel fully satisfied.

Chances are likely that even as I attempt to seek out joy I will still, quite often, actually deteriorate into the regular version of my worst self. I will imagine strangers are mad at me, I will police my friends' hunger—*But are you sure you don't need a snack?*—and I will become convinced that my husband changed the water pressure on the showerhead to spite me. I will fail to read school emails explaining that my son will be a social outcast unless I remind him that Tuesday is Crazy Sock Day. And certainly I will choose the loveliest moment on vacation or while out at a nice dinner to raise the difficult issue that could have waited. *Sorry, why did everyone stop having a good time?*

But even Saint Augustine knew that no matter what you survive—no matter how grateful you wish you were—you will still feel irritated or shruggy a lot of the time. "Everything, however wonderful, ends in boredom," he observed.

Joy is not a solution, not an answer, not a cure. But maybe it's a song—because even the deepest ache has a melody.

I heard that song again the other day when I was doing an interview with a woman whose daughter had died. She spent decades devoted to nonprofit work to help others afflicted with the same pain. But—wouldn't you know?—lately she finds herself writing juicy historical romance novels about Mennonites in possibly-more-than-hand-holding situations. I was *delighted* by this little revelation, and it reminded me again of the moment Frederick Buechner changed his mind about whether he was allowed to be joyful. His daughter was suffering with anorexia and he had laid down that devastating rule that he should suffer equally with her. He believed, as a parent, that his misery was useful and good and necessary. *I cannot survive if she does not. We are chained at the ankle.*

Eventually though, he decided, no, he was wrong. And then he seems to have given himself his own prescription for joy: he said that all of us have a kind of "sacred commission" to breathe free and bless our own lives. In the good times and bad, we must believe that we are becoming the type of people who hear a lifesaving word and may even be able to speak those words of hope to others.

Keep your ears open: perhaps a song is about to play.

"Never let us live with *amousia*," said the ever-insightful C. S. Lewis. It was something his own favorite teacher had repeated again and again, which meant: do not try to live without the Muses, without creative inspiration, without the ability to distinguish sound. Listen, really listen, with your whole being. "Without music," observed philosopher Friedrich Nietzsche, "life would be a mistake."

A couple of weeks ago, I went to a goodbye party for my friend Steven, who was moving away. One of the other guests at the party was an accomplished cellist. As a farewell gift, he composed and played a song.

"Steven sounds like this," said the cellist, introducing his composition. He glided his hands smoothly up and down the fingerboard in a peaceful melody. "But Caitlyn sounds a bit more like: FLANG FLANG BLEEEE. FLANG FLANG BLEEEE." He mashed the sides of his fists against the cello's neck and ground the strings with the bow, and it was horrible.

We all giggled, a little uncomfortable. Caitlyn was Steven's partner and the truth is, we were all sort of hoping they would break up. They had just never seemed well matched. But then, the cellist began to play. Steven's life as a song—both melodic and percussive—was beautiful. Later, I asked the musician about how brave he must have felt to reveal the difference between our friend and his terrible companion. He swore he didn't think her biographical song was all that bad because he knew that when he put the sounds together they would form a beautiful harmony.

"Yes, totally," I assured the cellist. "It was a gorgeous song. But they definitely need to break up. Caitlyn is such a FLANG FLANG BLEEEE person."

It reminds me of what Jack Black, as the heartbroken songwriter in the movie *The Holiday,* says as he considers opening himself up to someone new.

He looks over at his heart's desire sitting beside him at the piano. "If you were a melody . . ." he says, and then he plays the sweetest melancholy tune.

She grins.

"I used only the good notes," he says.

We want a life of only the good notes. That is the great siren song of positivity—despite the fact that our lives are evidence to the contrary. The grief and unending losses, the ordinary paper cuts and the deep, deep longings—perhaps that is why the ache so often becomes a song too. Because there are some truths we can only tell in a minor key.

Joy allows us to play all of the notes—both the sweetest tunes and the real *flang flang blee* situations.

That is not a glitch in our programming or a tear in the fabric of the universe. Each of us, no matter how undone we are before 7:00 A.M. and after 8 P.M., has a tremendous capacity for joy. And we will experience it mostly as a complete contradiction: as something we can turn toward and say, "Yes!" and something that we can do absolutely nothing to achieve. Sometimes we can dig them up and cling to our joys with our own two hands. And some will simply have to descend on us like a dove, like a mercy.

Joy might pop up, every now and again, in moments of our greatest undoing.

When I was talking to theologian Jerry Sittser, I asked him about what kind of person he needed to become to survive the death of his wife, mother, and child; he had begun a new life with a second marriage and lived beautifully, decades and decades *after* tragedy.

"I think you became very courageous," I observed.

"Have you ever read the novel *Hannah Coulter* by Wendell Berry?" he asked.

I shook my head.

"Hannah is a young woman in a small town in Kentucky, and she experiences the loss of a husband at a young age. And the author says of her, 'she came to the point where she realized that life itself was demanding life from her.' "

Life was demanding life.

Jerry paused. "I supposed I realized that life was requiring something of me." And so he got married for the second time, even though there are no second marriages, only a new marriage to a new person. He took a risk to love again, even though he knew that he would limp along as the walking wounded.

We have all met people who are done taking risks. Some of them are plenty comfortable. Others are simply too tired to enumerate the many, many kinds of physical, emotional, financial, and spiritual ways there are to be afraid. It would be easy to conclude that risk is simply fear by another name.

But what if the desire for joy doesn't give us another option?

"We must risk delight . . ." said the poet Jack Gilbert. "We must have the stubbornness to accept our gladness in the ruthless furnace of this world."

I don't think I would have become a joyful person if I had not had such an unlucky life, if I had not been forced into risk at every turn. But I have come to realize that the two are inseparable. Joy shows up when we are out on a limb.

A risky life is perhaps what George Bernard Shaw was describing when he promised himself he would be "thoroughly used up when I die." He wouldn't stop early. He wouldn't hoard his resources for later. He would act as if he were going to spend his last penny, like the retired sausage-maker, Charlie, using his remaining strength to love a stranger every day. No wonder Shaw concluded: "This is the true joy in life, being used for a purpose recognized by yourself as a mighty one."

Come nightfall, I will be tasked with the singular and mighty purpose of putting a boy to bed. Tonight, in the quiet of his room, he is busy assuring me that the bits of glass that

I am trying to pick off his side table are "surely diamonds" he has found in a nearby stream. Downstairs my husband is clanking around at the sink doing what remains of the dishes from one of my overly elaborate salads. There is nothing left to do except think about tomorrow's impossibilities and the early signs of hoarding this room seems to be pointing to . . .

"Do you have time to answer some of my bison's questions about politics?" asks Zach, yawning. I can barely see his face surfacing under three full duvet covers and a burrito blanket. His stuffies have been having a lot of existential quandaries lately, but these are the loose threads of the day, where we will find no end of needs to pray about, fears to spin up, and reasons to never climb out of the basement.

We can hide if we want to, but, most likely, tomorrow we will all need to take a chance.

That we might be delighted. That we might be grateful. That we might be more hopeful than we thought possible.

And when we're not, we can sing to joy: *come find me.*

ACKNOWLEDGMENTS

I took the long road to joy, and thank you to everyone and everything who helped me get here.

Lemurs. Family. Best Friends. Improv. Graveyards. Priests. Massage therapy. Duke basketball. Group texts. Weird days at work. Girls' weekends. Divinity school. Trash-talking. Trash walking. Largest statues. Anyone named Tom Holland. My son's freshly shampooed head.

Thank you especially to Whitney Frick and Hilary Redmon and Margaret Riley King for championing this book.

And thank you to the women in my life who convinced me that, well and truly, *there is more.*

ABOUT THE AUTHOR

KATE BOWLER is the four-time *New York Times* bestselling author of *Everything Happens for a Reason; No Cure for Being Human; Good Enough; The Lives We Actually Have; Have a Beautiful, Terrible Day; Blessed;* and *The Preacher's Wife*. She hosts the popular podcast *Everything Happens* and writes the Substack of the same name. A Duke University professor, she earned a master's of religion from Yale Divinity School and a PhD at Duke University.

katebowler.com
katebowler.substack.com
Facebook.com/katecbowler
Instagram and TikTok: @katecbowler

ABOUT THE TYPE

This book was set in Sabon, a typeface designed by the well-known German typographer Jan Tschichold (1902–74). Sabon's design is based upon the original letter forms of sixteenth-century French type designer Claude Garamond and was created specifically to be used for three sources: foundry type for hand composition, Linotype, and Monotype. Tschichold named his typeface for the famous Frankfurt typefounder Jacques Sabon (c. 1520–80).